P9-DMP-388

Tales from the Sooners Sideline

JAY C. UPCHURCH

Foreword by Barry Switzer

SportsPublishingLLC.com

ISBN-10: 1-59670-249-4
ISBN-13: 978-1-59670-249-3
ISBN: 1-58261-320-6 (hard cover)

Front cover photo by Ronald Martinez/Getty Images
Back cover photo by Shutterstock

Publishers: Peter L. Bannon and Joseph J. Bannon Sr.
Senior managing editor: Susan M. Moyer
Editor: Travis W. Moran
Art director: Dustin J. Hubbart
Cover design: Dustin J. Hubbart
Project manager: Kathryn R. Holleman
Photo editor: Erin Linden-Levy

Sports Publishing L.L.C.
804 North Neil Street
Champaign, IL 61820
Phone: 1-877-424-2665
Fax: 217-363-2073
www.SportsPublishingLLC.com

Printed in the United States of America

Library of Congress Cataloging-in-Publication Data

Upchurch, Jay C.
Tales from the sooners sideline / Jay C. Upchurch ; foreword by Barry Switzer.
    p. cm.
   ISBN-13: 978-1-59670-249-3 (soft cover : alk. paper)
   ISBN-10: 1-59670-249-4 (soft cover : alk. paper)
   ISBN-10: 1-58261-320-6 (hard cover : alk. paper)
    1. Oklahoma Sooners (Football team)--History. 2. University of Oklahoma--Football--History. I. Title.
   GV958.O4U73 2007
   796.332'630976637--dc22
                              2007016185

To Virgil and Jo Ellen, the most amazing parents a boy could ever ask for. Thanks for the love, guidance, and understanding—and most of all for the freedom that allowed me to choose my own path. To my brother, Gary—thank you for sharing the experience.

And to my son, Jacob Cole—welcome to the game of life. Live it passionately and with goodness in your heart.

Contents

Chapter One

From the birth of football in Norman to the arrival of the 1940s, there are tales of triumph, defeat, bedlam, All-Americans, stickers, spirit, titles, strays, lists, steers, and brawls.

Chapter Two

The decade that changed OU football forever, as Charles "Bud" Wilkinson arrives on campus to help chase away any signs of lingering mediocrity. There's Jim Tatum, George L. Cross, the Sisco incident, West Point action, eligible seamen, masterful lessons, mounds of fun, and General Jack.

Chapter Three

The Monster is born. On the verge of greatness during Bud Wilkinson's early years, the Sooners emerge on the national scene as one of the elite programs in the country. See this brave new world, the Great White Father, a kid named Vessels, the statement, national titles, the streak, the perfect quarterback, team unity, and tough love.

Chapter Four
THE 1960s 59

The end of a great era and the beginning of a new dawn. Experience both through the "58 Special," a visit from Jack, the end of the road, Sooner dreams, the Wicked Worm, a problem child, remembering the land run, the fourth-quarter class, Granny, and a true All-American.

Chapter Five
THE 1970s 85

The wishbone comes to town and national titles come with it. Live it up with popsicles and Gatorade, the departure of Little Red, the Game of the Century, the Selmon brothers, rolling over, Sooner Magic, good company, and a different kind of rug.

Chapter Six
THE 1980s 125

Barry Switzer helps bring home another title and then makes his exit. The post-disco era includes a man among boys, illegal procedure and the ponies, Big Marcus, hot water cornbread, answered prayers, a higher power, a kid named Boz, bad timing, and more Sooner Magic.

Chapter Seven
THE 1990s AND BEYOND 151

A tough decade begins. Still, there is sweet redemption, a crooner for the Sooners, the great crash, the walk, Cecil, a nice finish, the softer side, the turning point, and the runt.

Foreword

THERE IS A MAGIC about the University of Oklahoma football program that transcends time as it captures and holds the hearts of generation after generation of Sooner fans. It is a phenomenon made up of a million different stories that span more than a century of great teams, great players, and great moments.

The history is deep and rich, and the tradition is unmatched. Oklahoma football is one of the great enduring icons in collegiate athletics. From coast to coast and border to border, the Sooners have long represented a level of success that most schools can only imagine.

Many of the legendary and not-so-legendary characters whose faith, commitment, and determination helped shape OU's illustrious reputation come to life in this book through a series of colorful tales that recount humorous events, celebration and heartfelt emotion, as well as more weighty times. Their human side shines through in a way that is rarely shared beyond the inner circles of the Sooner family.

From humble beginnings and Bennie Owen providing the initial foundation to the birth of greatness with Bud Wilkinson to the program's recent resurgence under Bob Stoops, Oklahoma football has long been a benchmark for young men who strive for greatness, not only as individuals, but as a contributing piece of the overall puzzle.

There is a genuine sense of pride and camaraderie that is inherent among those who have worn the crimson and cream. To be a part of something so special is what every competitor, every coach dreams about.

My association with the Sooners and Oklahoma football has enriched my life and made for so many great memories.

To know Sooner football is to love it. In all of my experiences, there is nothing else quite like it.

Enjoy!

—BARRY SWITZER

Acknowledgments

THERE ARE ENOUGH STORIES—some new, some very familiar and some never before told—to write a series of books entitled *Tales from the Sooner Sideline.* The heroes and characters through the years are abundant; the emotions and drama, quite infamous. Finding just the right blend was the biggest challenge I faced in putting together this particular volume of tales.

The research involved was much more taxing and enlightening than I ever imagined. As much as I might have thought myself an "expert" on OU football history before this project, I have since come to realize and appreciate so very many chapters that did not previously exist for me. And there are many more waiting to be explored and told.

In my pursuit to write this book, I interviewed dozens of former (and current) players and coaches and many witnesses to the stories that unfold within these pages. I read books and studied articles and talked with other authors about their experiences in following the Sooners.

It was and is an amazing journey.

Finding a place to begin all of the thank-yous and acknowledgments I owe is difficult in itself, because so many people gave generously of their time to help piece all of this together. I suppose starting with the men whom this book is all about is as good a place as any. So here goes and please forgive me if anyone falls through the cracks.

Special thanks to the following OU players and coaches: Barth Walker, Gene Corrotto, Port Robertson, Frank "Pop" Ivy, Stan West, Norman McNabb, Bob Bodenhamer, Prentice Gautt, Clendon Thomas, Billy Vessels, Leon "Mule Train" Heath, Jimmy Harris, Merle Dinkins, Jerry Cross, Jakie Sandefer, Jerry Pettibone, Karl Milstead, Darrell Royal, Brewster Hobby, Bob Harris, Ronnie Fletcher, Steve Owens, Bobby Warmack, Steve Zabel, Mike Harper, J. D. Martin, Don Jimerson, Tinker Owens, Barry Switzer, Bobby Proctor, Keith Jackson, Merv Johnson, Greg Pruitt, Larry Lacewell, Uwe von Schamann, George Cumby, Jamelle Holieway, Brian Bosworth, Mike Vaughn, Billy Brooks, Sherwood Taylor, Sonny Brown, Paul Migliazzo, Gene Hochevar, Steve Davis, Scott Hill, Tim Lashar, Earl Johnson, Thomas Lott, Mike Gaddis, Cale Gundy, Spencer Tillman, James Allen, Bob Stoops, Torrance Marshall, Trent Smith, Roy Williams, Nate Hybl, Damian Mackey, Josh Norman, Quentin Griffin and Josh Heupel.

I would also like to thank the following people for their contributions: Joe Castiglione, Mike Treps, Mike Prusinski, Debbie Copp, Jay Wilkinson, Kirk Herbstreit, Ed Montgomery, Rob Collins, Kenny Mossman, Bob Barry Sr., J. Brent Clark, Al Eschbach, Ned Hockman, the University of Oklahoma Sports Information Department, University of Oklahoma yearbook archives, Western History Museum/University of Oklahoma Libraries, Jerry Laizure, John Keith, Terry Tush, Sissy Tubb, Clarke Stroud, Tony Vann, Brad McClure, Amber Friesen, Walter Cronkite, Ray Thurmond, and the late Charles R. Coe.

Research material also included:

Presidents Can't Punt by George Lynn Cross; *Bootlegger's Boy* by Barry Switzer; *Oklahoma Kickoff* by Harold Keith; *Sooner Century* by J. Brent Clark; *Sooners Illustrated* Magazine; *The Norman Transcript*; *The Anadarko Daily News*.

I appreciate the inspiration I have received from a great supporting cast during this process, as well as all of the helpful assistance from so many different sources. It's been a blast.

–JAY C. UPCHURCH

CHAPTER ONE

The Early Years

First Signs of Life

LONG BEFORE THE LIKES OF BUD WILKINSON, Barry Switzer, and Bob Stoops strolled the Oklahoma sidelines, the crimson and cream found itself under the direction of Bennie Owen, a legend in his own right. Owen was the fifth man to coach OU football, but it wasn't until he took over in 1905 that the Sooners actually became a program to be reckoned with.

Owen's first order of business was to install an aggressive offensive system built around speed and an advanced passing game that proved far superior to the more common grind-it-out strategy that required little imagination and even less finesse. Innovative thinking made Owen an offensive pioneer, and his team's results were proof—the Sooners rolled up more than 100 points on eight different occasions while eclipsing the 50-point mark another 31 times.

OU recorded four undefeated seasons during Owen's 22 years at the helm. Even so, most of Owen's teams labored in obscurity while schools from the Midwest and East Coast garnered most of the national attention. That all changed when Owen helped raise an unthinkable $350,000 to build a

32,000–seat stadium, which helped put the Sooners on the national map.

Owen retired with a record of 122-54-16 after the 1926 season. As a tribute to the longtime Sooner skipper, the field at Memorial Stadium was named after him.

Coach and Teacher

The football team was still in its infant stages when Oklahoma hired Vernon Parrington, an English professor, as its first full-time coach in 1897. Over the next four years, the Harvard graduate led the squad to a 9-2-1 mark.

Despite his success, Parrington was more interested in teaching, so he resigned his coaching position to do just that. But in 1908, he was fired when an investigation developed evidence that some faculty members were guilty of such serious offenses as dancing and smoking.

Parrington never coached again, but he went on to win the 1928 Pulitzer Prize for history while teaching at the University of Washington.

Tragedy to Triumph

With coach Bennie Owen confined to a hospital bed due to a hunting accident that resulted in the amputation of his right arm, team captain Bill Cross guided Oklahoma to a 29-0 victory over Epworth University on October 25, 1907. The Sooner quarterback led his team on three scoring drives, while making sure all aspects of the OU game plan ran smoothly in Owen's absence.

Nine days earlier, Owen had gone quail hunting with druggist John Barbour near Adkins Ford, just south of Norman on the South Canadian River. While loading their dogs and weapons onto Barbour's horse-drawn wagon, Owen's 12-gauge Winchester pump automatic shotgun accidentally discharged.

The blast struck Owen in the arm, severing an artery below his right shoulder.

In the ensuing hours, a local physician was unable to restore circulation, and the arm had to be removed. During his time in the hospital, it was reported that Owen expressed more concern about his absence from the OU football team than about the loss of his arm.

Shocked by the stunning news, Owen's squad dropped a 15-0 decision to Kansas three days after the acccident. It was the only game OU lost on it's home field in Norman during Owen's first seven years at the helm.

Amazingly, within two weeks Owen was back on the field coaching.

Inauspicious Beginning

In the fall of 1895, it was difficult to determine which was more fledgling—the young railroad town of Norman or the University of Oklahoma, founded only five years earlier. In any case, John A. Harts, also known as Jack, was determined to bring football to both. A former player at Winfield College in Kansas, he helped do just that by recruiting players for OU's first team.

The ever-determined Harts put together his makeshift football crew in local businessman Bud Risinger's Main Street barber shop. Those recruits, with Harts serving as both coach and captain, played their first game against a team from Oklahoma City on November 7 of that year.

Bedlam's Beginnings

Bedlam is defined by Webster as "a scene of wild uproar and confusion; a madhouse." It is the perfect description for the rivalry that has developed between Oklahoma and Oklahoma State over the last century.

Although the series was not called "Bedlam" until the 1950s, even from its earliest days, the rivalry has always lived up to its reputation.

Cross-state foes Oklahoma and Oklahoma A&M first met on a frigid November afternoon in 1904. The Rough Riders (they didn't become the Sooners until 1908) met the Aggies that day at Guthrie's Old Island Park, which was bordered by the banks of Cottonwood Creek.

Action was fettered by a stiff north wind so cold that players from both sides suffered frostbite by the conclusion of OU's 75-0 triumph, which included any number of unusual circumstances. The most bizarre occurred on an Aggie punt that was caught by the harsh winds and blown backwards into the icy waters of the nearby creek.

Because there were no end lines that dictated an out-of-bounds area, the ball remained in play as it bobbed up and down in front of a legion of players from both sides, most of whom were hesitant to go in after it.

OU's Ed Cook, however, did not fit into that group. Seeing a pair of Aggies, including lineman T. Becker Matthews, test the waters, Cook jumped in and was the first player to the ball. He quickly made his back to shore upon retrieving it and, once there, touched the ball into the end zone area for a Sooner score.

By the end of the day, every OU player had scored a touchdown. The 75-point margin of victory remains the largest in the series' 101-game history.

A Thorny Situation

During the early years of Oklahoma football, getting crunched by an opposing defender was sometimes the least of a player's worries. Many of the gridirons the teams played on were carved out of fields or pieces of open land that weren't conducive to football. Ball carriers often found themselves dodging potholes and an occasional rock or two.

But the biggest concern, according to OU quarterback Bill Cross, were the thickets of sand burrs.

During a game against Epworth College at Oklahoma City's Colcord Park, the burr situation was so serious that players from both sides were constantly holding up the action to pick the thorny objects from their legs and hands.

"The field was full of sand burrs. So was the ball. Nobody wanted to handle it," said Cross, describing the conditions of the 1907 contest.

Sooner Charlie Wantland said that it took him two years to remove all of the sand burrs from his back after he quit playing in 1908. He added, "Ball carriers braced themselves from falling down in order to avoid the painful burrs."

The First All-American

According to OU coach Bennie Owen, there were not enough positive adjectives to describe the talent Claude Reeds possessed on a football field. The 6-foot, 165-pound speedster could run, pass, block, kick and catch the ball with equal grace and agility. Reeds' performances were dominating as he helped lead the Sooners to their first unbeaten and untied season ever in 1911.

His career was marked by bone-crunching blocks, bullet passes that riddled opposing defenses and his incredible punting skills. But he is best remembered for a fake punt that he turned into a 70-yard touchdown run on November 27, 1913. On the play, Reeds wove his way back and forth across ankle-deep mud covering Fair Park Field, eluding numerous Colorado defenders en route to the end zone.

Observers on hand believed Reeds' jaunt through the thick slop to be almost 200 yards in all. OU beat the Buffs that day 14-3.

At the conclusion of his senior season in 1913, Reeds became the first OU football player to earn All-America honors.

Tradition of Spirit

The RUF/NEKS are a time-honored tradition at OU. The spirit group has been caretaker for the Sooner Schooner since its introduction in 1965, and its affiliation with the Sooner football program is one of historic distinction.

The RUF/NEKS, originally founded in 1915, came about almost by accident during a basketball game between Oklahoma and archrival Oklahoma A&M. During the heated contest, a number of rowdy OU football players began to incite several members in the crowd. Their spirited antics proved a bit much for one elderly female fan who shouted her disapproval, "Sit down and be quiet, you roughnecks!"

And so, the oldest men's collegiate pep group was born. The name was adopted by the organization and altered to RUF/NEKS. As the group became more defined with time, the RUF/NEKS evolved from basic cheerleading into a group that helped promote school spirit at other levels, including pregame bonfires and postgame celebrations.

Passing to the Crown

Bennie Owen had long preached the forward pass, but not until 1915 did he have the player who could utilize it fully. Spot Geyer was that player, and by the end of the Sooners' initial season in the Southwest Conference, he had matured into one of the best passers in the land.

Geyer helped lead OU to a perfect 10-0 record and the conference title. He threw for a school-record 288 yards in a victory over Kansas and kicked the extra point that was the difference in a 14-13 win against Texas.

The senior quarterback's celebrity grew tremendously on campus and throughout Norman, and he capped his career by earning All-America honors, making him only the second Sooner to achieve that status.

Too Hott to Handle

Long before Eufaula's Selmon brothers descended on Memorial Stadium with the heart and ferocity that helped earn the Sooners two national championships in the 1970s, the Hott brothers were all the rage in Norman. Sabert, Oliver and Willis Hott earned the nickname "The Terrible Hotts" for their spirited style of play.

Between the years 1910-16, at least one Hott brother favored the Sooner lineup with unparalleled fervor and mettle. Sabert, the eldest, also known as Old Sabe, played four seasons despite having only one eye, the other having been lost in a railroad accident some years earlier.

Younger brothers Willis and Oliver, nicknamed Big Hott and Little Hott, respectively, were among the most popular players on coach Bennie Owen's squads from 1913-16.

Fans became so enamored with the brothers that they came up with a special chant thanks to the help of OU's first yell-master, Leslie High.

It went something like this: "Big Hott! Little Hott! Red Hott! Too Hott! Woo!"

What's in a Name?

Lawrence Haskell was a well-known name around the Oklahoma campus for most of 30 years. Besides lettering in football and baseball for the Sooners from 1918-22, he served as head baseball coach and freshman football coach for his alma mater from 1927-41. And after serving in the navy during World War II, Haskell returned to OU as athletics director.

Jap, as he was known throughout his life, was the nickname he earned while growing up in the small Oklahoma town of Anadarko. As a teenager, Haskell would borrow his brother Pat's harness horse named Jasper W., along with his rubber-tired, maple-wheeled buggy. Young Haskell was seen so frequently in the company of the horse, the people of Anadarko referred to him by the horse's name, shortening the Jasper to Jap.

While athletic director, Haskell was credited with helping discover legendary OU football coach Charles "Bud" Wilkinson. The university named its new baseball field after Haskell in 1963, just months prior to his death.

Nice Stadium, Lousy Facilities

When Oklahoma poured almost $350,000 into the construction of a new 32,000-seat stadium in the 1920s, most people believed the university had elevated its athletic programs, especially football, to unthinkable heights. And in many ways, they were right.

Spectators traveled from near and far to watch Bennie Owen's Sooners perform on the gridiron. Memorial Stadium was beautifully displayed as the centerpiece of the ever-expanding campus, and it would one day be home to one of the greatest traditions in the annals of college football.

But for those players who initially put their talents on display at the venue, there was little to cheer about when it came to amenities. The locker rooms were dark and cramped, as were most of the facility's inner workings. One OU player described the players' quarters as less desirable than what he had experienced at his small high school back home.

While Owen was responsible for helping raise the money for the new stadium and building the Sooners into a vastly respected program, there was still room for major improvement. It would not come for another 10 years.

Oklahoma's Most Famous Dog

During the 1980s and '90s, Oklahoma debuted a new mascot for home basketball games. His name was "Top Daug," and his performances and antics became popular with Sooner fans, young and old.

But there was another dog in OU sports history that enjoyed unequaled popularity. Mex, a handsome tan and white terrier dressed in a red sweater and cap with a white embroidered "O," served as the school's original mascot from 1919-28. His familiar staccato bark accompanied Sooner touchdowns as well as runs scored at OU baseball games.

Prior to his career as a mascot, Mex was rescued by a U.S. Army field hospital unit in 1914 during the Mexican Revolution. Medic and soon-to-be OU student Mott Keyes found the dog among an abandoned litter of puppies near the Mexican border.

As mascot, Mex helped entertain spectators between quarters by catching hedge apples tossed to him by members of the Spirit Squad.

When Mex died on April 30, 1928, the entire university closed for his funeral. He was buried in a small casket under Memorial Stadium.

Three Captains from Caddo County

There are no documented records showing where team captains have come from over the years. But it is fairly safe to say few towns the size of Anadarko, Oklahoma, (population 6,000) produced as many Sooner captains.

Charles Ross Hume, Jap Haskell and Pete Hammert Jr. did their part to put the small Caddo County community on the map.

Interestingly enough, Hume's run as captain during the 1896 season was expunged from the records when officials determined the two games OU played that season were recorded only as exhibitions. Hume, who played quarterback, later became the first OU graduate.

Haskell captained the Sooners during the 1921 season, and he went on to become head baseball coach and freshman football coach at his alma mater in the late 1920s. In 1945, Haskell was hired as OU director of athletics.

Meanwhile, Hammert was a captain for Bennie Owen's 1923 OU squad.

Staggering Victory

When Adrian Lindsey took over in 1927, Oklahoma fans were unsure how the new coach would perform in the lingering shadow of legendary mentor Bennie Owen. And while the young Oklahoma native enjoyed a memorable debut—the Sooners defeated Amos Alonzo Stagg's powerful University of Chicago squad, 13-7—his four seasons at the helm proved mostly unproductive.

Lindsey's teams went 19-19-6 during that span, and Lewie Hardage followed with three more seasons of mediocrity. During an era when the Great Depression took its toll on the country, Oklahoma football fans didn't even have a football team to help them forget the hard times.

To worsen matters, by 1934, a major drought had turned parts of Oklahoma into a wasteland that became known as the Dust Bowl. While other elite teams were earning invitations to prestigious bowl games, the Sooners were again buried in obscurity—and dust.

Not until the 1990s did OU followers have as much to lament when it came to their football program.

No Strays Allowed

When OU officially made Mex the dog its mascot in 1919, one of his original duties was to chase stray dogs off of Boyd Field during game days. Located near a group of houses and without a surrounding fence, the football venue seemed like a magnet for curious animals, especially when the locals would gather to watch their favorite college team.

As a spectator, it was not unusual to see the feisty terrier nipping at the heels of a much larger canine, all while the

Sooners were calling signals and running plays somewhere nearby on the field.

It's All Relative

Leo, Al and Gene Corrotto, who hailed from Fort Smith, Arkansas, scripted their Sooner story in 1930s when the program was vying for national status. The strapping trio preceeded their cousins—Art and Bill Pansze—as members of OU's football program.

The Corrotto brothers arrived in Norman via a freight train in the summer of 1935 and wasted little time making their presence felt on Biff Jones' OU squad. At least, Al and Gene did. Leo, who had been one of the top kickers in the Southwest Conference as a freshman at Arkansas the previous season, found out the Razorbacks would not release his credits to allow him to play at OU. Instead of going to a junior college for a season, he returned home and soon after decided to quit playing football.

Al and Gene remained and became staples in the Sooners' double- and single-wing sets. The 5-foot-11, 168-pound Gene returned to action as right halfback after suffering a shoulder injury his freshman season, while Al excelled for three campaigns at blocking back and linebacker.

"It's funny because Leo was the best athlete out of the three of us, and he ended up not playing anymore," said Gene, who was co-captain with Earl Crowder on the OU squad that played in the 1939 Orange Bowl.

The Dreaded List

Biff Jones arrived in Norman after spending three tumultuous seasons at LSU, where he was best known for running Louisiana Gov. Huey P. Long out of his locker room at halftime of the 1934 LSU-Tulane game. Although Jones' Tigers went 20-5-5 during his time there, he decided the head coaching position at Oklahoma presented a new challenge.

Jones, a captain for the West Point football team during his collegiate playing days and a former army major, was hard working and well disciplined. He was a no-nonsense kind of coach, and he expected the same type of dedication from his players.

"He kind of ran the football team like it was army. He hardly ever spoke to the players and basically sat back and let his assistants do their work," said Barth "Jiggs" Walker, who played line for the Sooners from 1935-37. "When he wanted you to know something, it was posted on the bulletin board."

At the end of his initial spring practice as the Sooners were breaking camp and preparing to finish the school year, Jones posted a list of names on the infamous bulletin board with a note that read, "The following players will not return next season."

Jones and his staff had analyzed every player and every position that spring, weeding out a number of young men who did not fit into the future of the program, at least in their eyes.

"It was pretty scary walking up and looking at that list. Your heart was basically in your throat," added Walker, who made the cut. "Coach Jones was sort of aloof, but he really knew his football. I actually believe he was the beginning of the turnaround of Oklahoma football."

Teammate Gene Corrotto agreed: "Biff Jones is the man responsible for reorganizing the OU football program and pointing it in the right direction for those who followed."

Jones stayed only two seasons at OU, going 9-6-3 in the process. He went on to coach Nebraska and West Point before retiring with a career mark of 87-33-14.

And That's the Way It Is

Even before Oklahoma football became decorated with icons such as Bud Wilkinson, Billy Vessels, Barry Switzer and

Billy Sims, the Sooners had at least one brush with greatness. Even though it happened years before the man grew into legend.

Prior to the 1937 football season, WKY radio in Oklahoma City hired a young journalist by the name of Walter Cronkite to do its play-by-play commentary. The company that owned WKY had signed an exclusive contract to broadcast Sooner games that season, and it wasted no expense promoting its new radio team of Cronkite, Wray Dudley and Tom Churchill.

"It was most enjoyable," Cronkite once said. "I wasn't that long out of college myself. Of course, my association with the students was not extensive, because most of the time I was with the football team and the coaching staff.

"It was just the beginning of Oklahoma's surge into national prominence. It was a very exciting season."

Even though Cronkite remembers his first OU broadcast as "disastrous," he slowly became the voice of the Sooners as coach Tom Stidham's team forged a 5-2-2 record that included back-to-back ties with Texas and Nebraska and a 16-0 victory over Oklahoma State.

"I enjoyed that year at OU a great deal. It was great fun, but I didn't think it was a career," Cronkite offered. "It never occurred to me to make a career out of sports reporting."

After the '37 campaign, Cronkite decided to take a job with Braniff Airlines, and he eventually went on to become the most famous anchorman in television history.

Hey, Cactus Face

Arkansas native Gilford Duggan was a two-time All-Conference selection and a 1939 All-America tackle for the Sooners. Duggan earned the nickname "Cactus Face" due to the fact he almost always had a wiry three-day growth going. Teammate Gene Corrotto slapped the prickly nickname on Duggan after hearing it on the Jack Benny radio show late one night.

The 1939 Orange Bowl team. *Photo courtesy of the University of Oklahoma*

It was a great look for game days and probably served to provide Duggan with a more menacing appearance. But he usually broke out the razor on Saturday nights after games when it was fashionable to pursue young ladies at Rickner's bookstore-beer garden-soda fountain or the infamous Town Tavern on Campus Corner.

Steer Wrestling Sooner

The Oklahoma-Texas football rivalry took on monumental status long before the game became an annual tradition in Dallas and despite the fact that the Longhorns won 21 of the first 34 meetings. Both schools promoted the game with equal fervor, and the local press was quick to fan the flames that made

the game one of the most hotly contested in the country each season.

The *Norman Transcript* newspaper did its part to create a little added tension between the two teams when it ran a photo of Oklahoma lineman Barth Walker wrestling a Bevo lookalike to the ground prior to the 1937 showdown. Texas fans did not find a photo of their mascot being manhandled by a Sooner too amusing.

"Everybody kidded me about that picture. It was rather humorous, but I think it helped promote the game at a time when our program was getting back on its feet after some fairly lean years," explained Walker.

The game ended in a 7-7 tie.

The Orange Brawl

Oklahoma's defense had surrendered only 12 points during the entire 1938 regular season en route to a perfect 10-0 record. Defensive back Waddy Young, recognized as one of the best athletes on campus, spearheaded the Sooners' stingy attack as he became the program's first consensus All-American.

As a reward for their efforts, coach Tom Stidham's Sooners earned a trip to the 1939 Orange Bowl, their first ever postseason game. Winner of 14 straight games overall, OU might have been favored to beat Major Bob Neyland's undefeated Tennessee Volunteers if not for a rash of injuries that depleted its starting lineup.

The Sooners entered the contest missing starters Bill Jennings (broken leg), Howard "Red Dog" McCarty (broken thigh), Jerry Bolton (knee), Cliff Speegle (knee) and Steven Wood (knee). To make matters worse, both Cactus Face Duggan and Ralph Stevenson were ejected from the game for fighting in the first quarter.

And it didn't end there. Two minutes into the game, starting blocking back Earl Crowder was temporarily knocked unconscious, and he was unable to recover in time to be effective.

"It was awful. We had so many players injured over the latter part of the season that we were playing a lot of guys from our second team," said halfback Gene Corrotto. "I don't want to make excuses, but remember we only had a 40-man roster and most of the starters went both ways. So, you lose a guy, you lost him on both sides of the ball."

OU managed only 81 total yards, while Tennessee double-teamed Young most of the game and churned up almost 270 yards against the Sooner defense. The game was marred by over 200 yards in penalties as the Vols ran away to a 17-0 victory in Miami.

The contest was so rowdy that the headline in a Miami newspaper the following day read: "Orange Brawl."

It would be eight seasons before the Sooners returned to a bowl game.

CHAPTER TWO

The 1940s

Indian Jack

EVEN THOUGH LONGTIME COACH BENNIE OWEN had helped the Sooners devise a fairly effective passing attack during the early part of the century, OU fans had never seen the likes of Jack Jacobs when it came to throwing the football.

Jacobs, whose nickname was Indian Jack, was the proud owner of a rifle arm and quick wits. His speed and scrambling ability gave opposing defenses fits and earned him All-Big Six honors as a senior in 1941. He was also known for his punting ability, and he best demonstrated that during a game against Santa Clara at Memorial Stadium in his final season.

The Sooners were clinging to an 8-6 lead and pinned deep in their own end of the field when they were forced to kick. A slight wind was hitting Jacobs in the face as he retreated into punt formation, and he noticed the Santa Clara return man positioned very shallow in the secondary. Jacobs playfully motioned the player to move back, but he was not budging.

Jacobs shook his head and proceeded to boot a spiraling ball that cut through the October winds and did not stop until it had bounced and rolled inside the Santa Clara 10-yard line, finally covering a total of 85 yards. The OU defense subsequently held the Broncos, took over possession and scored the clinching touchdown in a 16-6 victory.

The Sooners were 18-8-1 during Jacobs' three seasons under center.

Big Red

Dewey Luster, who had spent most of the previous 24 years at OU as either a player, assistant coach or administrator, revealed a somewhat eccentric side when he took over as head coach in 1941. Nicknamed "Snorter" from his days as a lightweight boxer, Luster was bent on returning the Sooners to the glory years of an earlier period.

During his one short stint away from Norman, while studying law at Columbia University, Luster joined the New York Giants' staff as an apprentice and learned all about the revolutionary "A" formation that was all the rage in the NFL.

Luster deployed the "A" over his five seasons at the OU helm and saw his Sooners produce three highly successful campaigns. It was during that time the term "Big Red" became synonymous with OU football, thanks to Luster's penchant for favoring his junior and senior players over the team's less experienced players. As a result, the upperclassmen became known as Luster's "Big Red."

Death of a Sooner Hero

World War II cut a decided swath through college campuses in the months and years after the Japanese attack on Pearl Harbor and the United States' alliance with the Allied Forces. Many student athletes joined various branches of the service to fight for their country and world freedom.

Among those was OU's first ever consensus All-American, Roland "Waddy" Young, a strapping young buck who became a U.S. Air Force pilot and flew dozens of missions over Japan and Europe. Major Young and his flight crew were highly decorated for their unforgettable heroics. Unfortunately, they all lost their lives on a bombing mission just months before the conclusion of the war in 1945.

The news of Young's death hit Norman on a cold January day.

"When you met Waddy you could tell right away he was a leader. His teammates looked up to him with great respect," said former teammate Barth Walker. "He always carried himself well, and that showed on the football field and in life. I know when I heard about him being killed during the war, you just have to cry sometimes.

"It was just such a waste for a young man of that quality—he was an outstanding person—to be lost in such a way. I think about him often."

Game Film

When Bud Wilkinson initially approached Ned Hockman about filming the Sooners' football games in 1949, it figured to be a short-lived partnership, at best. Hockman was head of the OU Film Department, and spare time was something he did not have a lot of.

When he retired from OU in the mid-1980s, Hockman had filmed almost four full decades of OU games, beginning on October 2, 1948, and ending on November 19, 1987.

"Guess it worked out a little better than either of us originally expected," laughed Hockman.

Red River Rivalry

The best rivalry in college football. That's how the traditional October battle between Red River Rivals Oklahoma and Texas has been described. The series began in 1900 and moved permanently to its neutral site in Dallas in 1929.

Bud Wilkinson. *Photo courtesy of the University of Oklahoma*

Starting in 1941, the Golden Hat was awarded to the annual OU-Texas winner, and it has criss-crossed back and forth over the Red River 19 times since then.

An excerpt from the 2000 OU-Texas official game program, written by Jay C. Upchurch, reads:

Indelible images in every direction, beginning with an equally divided sea of crimson and burnt orange splashed against a backdrop that fuses a carnival atmosphere with the drama of athletic competition. Colorful characters, unbridled emotion, blaring rhetoric and heroic feats, all jammed into a coliseum setting and played out with unequaled pageantry.

Throw in a degree of contempt that can only be measured in decibels and a history of no-holds-barred, knock-down-drag-out feuding that runs a century deep, and it becomes quite clear this is a rivalry of paramount proportions.

It's Dallas, Texas. It's the Cotton Bowl. It's the Red River War.

This is Oklahoma vs. Texas, and it is a defining staple of college football.

The Longest Return

Midway through the 1945 season, a young Oklahoma team was showing signs of maturing as it headed to Manhattan, Kansas, for a game with Kansas State. Unfortunately that same week, head coach Snorter Luster's mother passed away, and he left the team to attend her funeral.

The Wildcats were considered the doormat of the Big Six, so the Sooners blew through preparations and arrived in Manhattan less focused than necessary. Luster joined the team late in the week, but his mind was not exactly on football, either.

But it was about to be. Kansas State dominated the favored Sooners during the opening half, scoring twice on buck-lateral option pass plays that helped them forge a 13-0 halftime lead.

A dazed OU team tried to gather itself in the locker room, but Luster was too embarrassed to join them. The Sooners went back out with the motivation that winning for Luster would provide a big shot in the arm.

OU began picking apart the K-State defense and dominating on both sides of the ball. The biggest play of the second half, during which the Sooners outscored the Wildcats 41-0, came when El Reno, Oklahoma, native Al Needs intercepted a pass three yards deep in the end zone and returned it for a touchdown.

Sprint and FADADA

Just call them the welcoming committee. But in reality, the RUF/NEKS are much more. Well before Oklahoma football became a symbol of success in the world of collegiate athletics, the OU spirit group had entrenched itself as part of the growing tradition.

The RUF/NEKS are visible every Saturday at Memorial Stadium as they take the point when the team runs onto the field. Members of the group sprint the length of the field with OU flags flying high and come to a sliding halt near the north goal post. Once there, amid shotgun blasts and a frenzied crowd, the RUF/NEKS chant the FADADA, which is believed to bring the Sooners good luck.

Working and Playing

Prior to the 1949 season, Oklahoma began renovations on Memorial Stadium. Plans included the addition of the northern grandstand and a new press box. Construction crews worked long hours in order to complete the project on time, and they got a little help from an unlikely source.

Several OU football players, needing jobs for the summer, joined the work force on the renovations. Among those who rolled up their sleeves with the construction crews were Dick Bowman, Bob Bodenhamer and Leon Manley.

"Leon was married at the time and he needed the money to help support his family," remembered former teammate Norman McNabb. "He was big and strong and he could push a two-wheeled buggy full of concrete around the construction site like it was nothing. Not only was he a fine football player, but he and some others literally helped build the place we played in."

Wanna Play Some Ball?

Upon his arrival on campus, new coach Jim Tatum wasted little time initiating a full-scale recruiting assault that herded as many potential players through a calculated evaluation process as possible. Spring practice of 1946 resembled an army boot camp with dozens of prospects shipped in and out on a weekly basis.

Tatum's staff kept notes when individual recruits distinguished themselves in some manner during workouts. They did the same thing during summer practice, which Tatum figured would give him another chance to determine the best talent for his squad.

"Tatum had them going around the clock. Anyone he had heard about from coast to coast found their way to campus and tried out for the team," said Norman McNabb, who played line at OU from 1946-50. "It was beyond your imagination the way he had potential players running in and out of those camps."

With so many players to chose from, it was no wonder the Sooners were able to field a highly competitive team that fall. Tatum's first and only OU squad finished 8-3 and earned the program's first trip to a bowl game in almost a decade.

Rain Can't Stop These Guys, Can It?

Oklahoma began the 1949 season with a rain-delayed opener in Chestnut Hill, Massachusetts, against a fledgling Boston College team that featured defensive star Art Donovan. The game was supposed to be played on a Friday night at Braves Field, but torrential rains made conditions unplayable.

"I'm not sure I'd ever seen it rain like that before or since.

The field was four or five inches under water by the time we were supposed to play," said lineman Stan West.

Bud Wilkinson's Sooners were suited up and awaiting the go-ahead on when they could begin pregame warmups when word came down from Boston College officials that the game was being postponed until Saturday night. The decision created more than a few problems for the Sooners, who had already checked out of their hotel rooms and chartered a flight back to Oklahoma late that night.

"Coach Wilkinson came in and told us the game was rained out, which made for some unusual circumstances," said senior Bob Bodenhamer.

The team returned to the hotel only to discover the New York Yankees, who were in town for a weekend series with Boston, had already been booked into their rooms. Fortunately, Wilkinson was able to work a deal for some other rooms.

The rain finally stopped that evening, and the following day presented perfect weather conditions. The field had drained amazingly well, and the Sooners took advantage by rolling up a 46-0 victory.

Have an "Aw-pull"

There were times when Jim Tatum's North Carolina accent gave the English language new meaning. Occasionally, his players would have to recount Tatum's locker room chats just to make sure they all understood exactly what he was talking about.

The Oklahoma coach was fond of giving each of his players a shiny red apple the night before every game. It became his pregame ritual throughout the 1946 season.

"Coach Tatum would say, 'Have an aw-pull' in his southern accent and then he'd wish you good luck for the game," explained lineman Wade Walker, who also played football for Tatum at the Jacksonville Naval Air Station during World War II. "It was something I think we all came to expect and appreciate."

Midnight Swim

The golf course, located in and around the OU Duck Pond, provided a cool place to hang out on hot autumn evenings. In fact, many of the Sooner football players were regular visitors there since it was located only a stone's throw away from their living quarters at Jefferson House.

One evening, Buddy Jones and Jim Acree decided to retrieve some golf balls from the pond near one of the par-three greens. Jones stayed ashore while Acree took his ROTC uniform off, laid it on the green and made his way into the water to begin the search.

Every time Acree found a ball he would toss it to Jones, who placed it in a long athletic sock. A few minutes into their little recovery mission, someone with a flashlight came walking toward the pond with a dog. Thinking it might be the police, Jones sprinted back to Jeff House, leaving Acree and the golf balls behind.

Acree, meanwhile, swam under the branches of a large willow tree and waited. Turned out the person with the flashlight was out gigging frogs, but his plans were altered when he noticed what looked like a body floating under a nearby tree. Alarmed, he took off to report what he had seen.

Too far away to retrieve his uniform, Acree exited the water and ran back to his room, where he got in bed and acted as if everything was normal. At the same time, the police made their way to the pond at the instruction of the frog gigger.

But they found no body, only an ROTC uniform and a sock full of golf balls. There was no name on the uniform, but it had a size 17 neck, which was evidence that it probably belonged to a football player.

The police headed over to the Jeff House and began asking around to see who was missing the uniform. But no one admitted to its ownership.

Finally, they came to Acree's room, and he gave them the same answer as everybody else. The main officer then told the players about the report of a body floating in the duck pond, to which Acree replied:

"I can assure you there is no body floating around down there."

Oops.

Siscoed in Texas

All of Oklahoma's pregame focus was on Texas quarterback Bobby Layne, but by the end of the 1947 Red River battle between the Sooners and Longhorns, all of the talk (and anger) centered around one particular official named Jack Sisco.

Many OU fans were outraged by a trio of controversial calls that altered the game tremendously, including a touchdown at the end of the first half that gave Texas the lead for good. The play happened on the south end of the Cotton Bowl, right in front of the Oklahoma fans.

In the moments following the controversial touchdown, beverage bottles came raining out of the stands, aimed mostly at Mr. Sisco.

"The quarterback's knee clearly touched the ground before he pitched to the kid who scored. It was one of several questionable calls that definitely made a difference in the game," explained OU linebacker Bob Bodenhamer. "We might not have won the game anyway, because Texas was probably the better team, but you hate to see it decided the way it was."

By the time Texas put the finishing touches on a 34-14 victory, Sisco and the rest of the officiating crew had to be escorted from the field and the stadium.

The bottle-throwing incident had also created major concerns. That game helped perpetrate the removal of glass containers of any kind at college venues.

Meanwhile, the word "Siscoed" became a verb back in Oklahoma.

Sideline Antics

According to many of his players, Jim Tatum had an eye for talent and the smarts to get the job done as a head coach. He proved that during his lone campaign at Oklahoma when his Sooners won eight times, including an impressive 34-13 decision over North Carolina State in the 1947 Gator Bowl.

Some would even say Tatum was maybe too focused on the task at hand. In fact, he became so engrossed in the action during games that he barely noticed his surroundings.

A perfect example was the Sooners' 1946 season-opening game against Army at West Point. During the contest, halfback Charlie Sarratt had injured his ankle and was sitting on the bench with his foot in a bucket of ice water. Tatum, pacing the sideline after a controversial call had gone against his team, picked Sarratt's foot out of the bucket, took a drink of the sweaty cocktail and stuck the foot back in, all in one swift motion.

The incident had OU's players rolling in laughter, but Tatum never blinked.

"I don't even think he realized what he'd done," said lineman Norman McNabb. "That's just how into the game he really was. His total focus was on what was happening to his team on the field."

Tommy's Sister

From 1947 to 1960, Oklahoma native Maria Tallchief was among the most recognized dancers in the world. In the 1950s, at the height of her career, she became America's preeminent dancer, a prima ballerina. President Dwight Eisenhower declared her "Woman of the Year" for 1953, and she remained in the public spotlight well into the 1960s.

Back in Norman, an ex-marine by the name of Tommy Tallchief turned out to be an All-Big Seven Conference football player for Oklahoma during the 1945 season. Despite his efforts on the gridiron, he never reached the notoriety level achieved by his famous sister.

More from West Point

Prior to OU's season-opening game with Army, coach Jim Tatum did everything imaginable to give his team an emotional edge. He talked about how the Sooners weren't getting any respect from the Cadets and how the East Coast media wasn't giving them any kind of chance to win that day.

Army was coming off of consecutive undefeated seasons, and its starting backfield included All-Americans Doc Blanchard and Glen Davis. Among the fans in Yankee Stadium that day was President Harry Truman, who proved to be the ultimate trump card for Tatum's motivational speech.

"The game started late due to the president's arrival, and Coach Tatum had us convinced that even President Truman was pulling against us," said All-America tackle Wade Walker.

"He was a character, a real motivator. He had us ready to run through a brick wall by the time we left the locker room."

Despite Tatum's moving pregame oration, the Cadets snapped a 7-7 tie with a pair of second-half touchdowns that carried them to a 21-7 victory.

Busy Boy

A four-year starter at Oklahoma, Darrell Royal capped a stellar career by earning All-America honors as a senior in 1949. After briefly testing his skills at the professional level, the Hollis, Oklahoma, native turned to coaching, where he would one day become a legendary figure at the University of Texas.

But long before Royal became a Longhorn he found himself zig-zagging across the country for a variety of coaching positions. At one point, Royal made eight stops in seven years.

It went something like this: Took the head job at El Reno (Oklahoma) High School, but left after two weeks when North Carolina State called; served one season as an assistant with the Wolfpack before taking a similar position at Mississippi State; returned to Oklahoma for an assistant position at Tulsa and after one season, returned to Mississippi State for the head job; the following season, Royal went to the Canadian Football League as a head coach and then got the job at Washington, where he also spent just one season before going to Texas.

Stinky Situation

Oklahoma had just defeated North Carolina 14-6 in the 1949 Sugar Bowl when the Sooners boarded a flight bound from New Orleans to Oklahoma City. For many members of Bud Wilkinson's squad, it was a time to celebrate and let off a little steam by partaking of an alcoholic beverage or two.

An hour or so and a few drinks into the flight, Jess Trotter needed to make a pit stop in the restroom. His timing could not have been worse.

Just as Trotter was taking care of business, the plane hit a vacuum air pocket in the clouds and plummeted several hundred feet in a matter of seconds. In the cabin, cocktail glasses and just about everything else that wasn't tied down went flying. In the restroom, Trotter had other problems.

"When that plane dropped like that, stuff came flying out of that john," said Norman McNabb. "Unfortunately, it got all over Jess. He stunk so badly that no one wanted to sit anywhere near him the rest of the flight. It was funny and sad at the same time."

Eligible Seamen

The 1945 season featured more than a few twists and turns as World War II came to a halt and the world readied for peace. The Oklahoma football team struggled to a 5-5 mark that fall with a young lineup that was minus several key players who were still serving active duty.

But that did not mean the Sooners were without any military personnel on their roster. A naval V-12 exemption allowed U.S. Naval personnel to participate at their base school, meaning sailors from the North and South bases at OU could play for Snorter Luster's team that season.

Several men who had been members of other college programs prior to their entering the military, went out for football at OU, including Ernie Davis, Elmer Friday and Gene Preston.

Are You the New Player?

In the days that followed after Jim Tatum was hired as head football coach at Oklahoma, he and assistant Bud Wilkinson found themselves staying in the athletic director Jap Haskell's basement—at least until they could find their own quarters.

One evening in Haskell's den, Tatum was greeting a handful of player prospects when one of the young lads asked Wilkinson what position he played.

"That wasn't unusual. Coach Wilkinson looked younger than a lot of the guys who were coming back to play college ball that year," offered Wade Walker.

Fact was, Wilkinson had been a two-time All-America performer at Minnesota during his collegiate playing days in the mid-1930s. After his senior season, he led the College All-Star Team to a 7-0 victory in its annual exhibition game with the NFL champions. In this case, it was the Green Bay Packers.

Running in the Red

Oklahoma was so bent on having a championship-caliber football program that it pretty much gave Jim Tatum a blank check when he arrived on campus. It wasn't that OU was paying its new coach tons of money, but he had the authority to buy anything he deemed critical to the success of his team.

That fact proved to be the undoing of athletic director Jap Haskell, who found his department running in serious debt by the end of the 1946-47 school year. Tatum had spent the Sooners into debt even though his team had revived serious interest in fans.

One of the major expenditures Tatum was responsible for was the way his team traveled—always taking two airplanes to away games.

"He split the team up and had us fly on two different planes, because he said if one plane went down, we could still play the game with the guys on the other plane," said lineman Norman McNabb. "Coach Tatum sometimes had an interesting way of looking at things."

When the '46 season concluded, Tatum approached OU President George L. Cross about a possible raise and contract extension. At the same time, he was talking to Maryland about its head coaching job. Cross' first move was to fortify the university's relationship with Wilkinson. OU felt very secure in promoting its top assistant if negotiations fell through with Tatum.

Because of the money problems, Cross did not enthusiastically pursue Tatum, and Tatum eventually took the

Maryland job. Wilkinson was hired as OU's new head coach in late January 1947.

Wilkinson Gives Masterful Lesson

During the early portion of Bud Wilkinson's legendary stint as head football coach at Oklahoma, he spent much of his spare time relaxing on the golf course. Wilkinson's regular group included two-time conference golf champ Charlie Coe. The two became fast friends during Coe's final two seasons at OU.

One summer afternoon in 1948, Wilkinson quizzed Coe about his concentration level and how he could further improve his game. An in-depth conversation ensued, and by the time Wilkinson finished, Coe had decided to dedicate himself more fully to every single shot, no matter how simple.

"Bud made me realize that if I concentrated with the same intensity on every shot I could greatly improve my game," Coe said, "I knew concentration was critical, but his advice helped me take my game to another level."

A year later, Coe won the first of his two U.S. Amateur Championships, and he went on to capture countless other tournament titles and play in the Masters 19 times, more than any other amateur in history.

Coe would later say he never forgot the advice of an old football coach.

Mounds of Fun

It's rare that a defensive player gets a chance to score a touchdown, and linebacker Bob Bodenhamer had already seen one such opportunity ripped from his grasp. It happened when he intercepted a pass against Kansas during the 1948 season and returned it for what he thought was his first career TD.

But Bodenhamer's roommate Dean Smith was called for clipping on the return, thus nullifying the ensuing celebration.

This time would be different, Bodenhamer must have thought as he picked off a pass against Boston College in the flat and had nothing but clear sailing to the end zone. No blocks were necessary, just trot along and watch Bodenhamer take it to the house.

Well, the game was being played at Braves Field, which served as the home of the Boston Braves baseball team. The yard was transformed into a football field for the OU-Boston College game, but the pitcher's mound remained intact near the five-yard line.

"I knew it was there because I had seen it before the game and during the game," admitted Bodenhamer.

"But as I was running, I wasn't thinking about anything but scoring. I had forgotten the mound was at that end of the field."

Just three steps shy of paydirt, Bodenhamer's dreams of a touchdown came to a stumbling halt, thwarted by a simple hill of dirt.

"It was embarrassing because there was no one near me," laughed Bodenhamer. "It took a while to get over because my teammates ribbed me pretty good for a long time."

Fortunately, the Sooners did not need the extra touchdown. They beat Boston College that night, 46-0.

Hands of Stone

Before Billy Vessels, Leon Heath, Buck McPhail, Tommy McDonald and Clendon Thomas there was George Thomas, whose performance during the 1948 and 1949 seasons was good enough to lead the conference in rushing. Thomas' running skills also earned him All-America honors as a senior.

His one weakness? Bad hands.

Thomas struggled to catch the ball out of the backfield, and as a result, he caught only five passes his entire college career.

"George was a helluva runner, but you had to hand it to him because he had hands like rocks," said teammate Stan West.

Basic Strategy

From the moment he took over as head coach at Oklahoma, Bud Wilkinson demanded nothing less than perfection from his players. Like Jim Tatum, he ran a well-disciplined camp that thrived on work ethic and smarts. Wilkinson implemented the Split-T offense and kept his players fresh by rotating his first and second teams in and out of contests.

His strategy was designed around wearing the opponent down and gaining an advantage that could be exploited in the second half. Wilkinson's favorite saying before every game: "We're going to pour the pine to them and wear them down physically, then win the game in the fourth quarter."

General Jack

No one was better at running the Split-T formation than Oklahoma quarterback Jack Mitchell. His field leadership earned him the nickname "General Jack," and opponents knew him as "Smiling Jack" because of the smile he always seemed to wear during games.

Mitchell was also a good punt returner, which like quarterback is a position that usually requires speed. That's the mystery of Mr. Mitchell.

"He was the slowest, most effective runner I ever saw," said All-America lineman Stan West. "Hell, Jack couldn't outrun me or anyone else on the team."

But during his two seasons as starting quarterback (1946-47), Mitchell produced a record of 18-3-1. And in 1949 when he moved to running back so Darrell Royal could call signals, the Sooners went 11-0.

"Jack just knew how to make people miss. It's hard to explain because he was so slow, but he was very successful," added teammate Norman McNabb.

CHAPTER THREE

The 1950s

The Great White Father

TALL AND DISTINGUISHED with silver-dusted hair and almost always wearing a well-tailored suit, Bud Wilkinson was so revered, so adored, that his presence basically stopped traffic wherever he went on campus and throughout the college community of Norman. Even his players viewed Wilkinson as unapproachable at times. "God-like" was his image, according to one former player.

"People were in awe of Coach Wilkinson. I know I was," said Jimmy Harris, who played quarterback at OU from 1954-56. "There was just something special about the man, the way he carried himself and spoke. I've never known anyone else like him."

It Begins

Oklahoma had won the national title in 1950 and had become a perennial powerhouse during Bud Wilkinson's first six seasons, but that paled in comparison to the successful journey the Sooners were about to embark on in 1953.

A loss to Notre Dame in the season opener and a tie against Pittsburgh preceded the first nationally televised Oklahoma-Texas game. Little did anybody know that the Sooners' 19-14 victory over the Longhorns on October 10 would be the beginning of a historic 47-game winning streak.

Wilkinson's squad won its final nine games in '53 and did not lose again until November 16, 1957, when Notre Dame earned a 7-0 decision in Norman.

"That's one of the most impressive accomplishments in sports history," said Barry Switzer, looking back on the career of Wilkinson. "To go four seasons without a loss is a record that won't be broken, at least not at that level."

Always Discreet

Dressing down players in practice or during a game simply wasn't Bud Wilkinson's style. Even when emotions ran hot, OU's coach had his own method of addressing problems dealing with individual players, and he almost always executed it with discretion.

"Coach Wilkinson could be both critical and encouraging, but he always did it privately," said All-America running back Clendon Thomas. "He'd pull you off to the side and guys didn't know if he was ripping you or complimenting you. Coach never embarrassed a player in front of the team."

That was always Wilkinson's philosophy. He remained on an even keel at all times.

"I never heard him raise his voice," offered Wade Walker.

"It wasn't that he never showed emotion—he did. But it was usually from a positive standpoint."

A Little Bedlam Fun

Tommy McDonald and Clendon Thomas not only shared the distinction of being part of the Sooners' starting 1956 backfield, but during that season the duo accounted for 38 touchdowns. As OU's season wound down, McDonald and Thomas were both in position to lead the country in scoring.

"It was very competitive because both Tommy and myself wanted the ball," offered Thomas. "But it was always a friendly competition. The bottom line was we both wanted what was best for the team."

Thomas had edged in front of McDonald by one touchdown during what would be a 53-0 victory over Oklahoma State in the regular-season finale. The Sooners were knocking on the door late when right tackle Ed Gray informed quarterback Jimmy Harris in the huddle that he had never scored a touchdown. In an unusual move, Thomas secretly switched places with Gray, who received the handoff on the next play and plunged into the end zone.

"That was great. Wilkinson thought it was a hoot—he got a really big kick out of that play," added Thomas, who wound up as the nation's leading scorer.

Better on Defense?

Any chance Oklahoma's first Heisman Trophy winner was actually a better defender than ball carrier? Maybe so.

According to those men who played with and coached Billy Vessels, he possessed as many skills on the other side of the ball as he did in the backfield.

"Vessels was tough and he knew how to play defense. What he did running with the ball speaks for itself, but he certainly was not shy about dishing it out on defense," said teammate Norman McNabb.

Brave New World

On October 21, 1950, Hoyt Givens and Harold Robinson, two young Kansas State recruits, became the first African-American players to participate in a game at Memorial Stadium.

The Sooners won easily that day, 58-0, but the color line had been challenged and the future would hold more changes.

"Kansas State was the first school in the Big Seven that played black kids. That showed a lot of foresight on their part," said OU lineman Norman McNabb. "It was unusual, but I don't think too many guys on our team gave it a second thought. There certainly weren't any incidents on the field."

A Kid Named Vessels

Fast, strong, intelligent—Billy Vessels had it all. And he used it all brilliantly during his collegiate career at Oklahoma. The Cleveland, Oklahoma, native was the ultimate football player, excelling on defense as well as on offense.

But it was his ball-carrying abilities and his break-away speed that helped etch his name alongside the greatest running backs in history.

"Billy Vessels was beautiful to watch. He just knew what to do when he got the ball," OU coach Bud Wilkinson once said.

As a sophomore, Vessels helped lead the Sooners to the 1950 national championship, rolling up 870 rushing yards while producing clutch performances against Texas, Texas A&M and Nebraska.

After a knee injury ended his junior season prematurely, Vessels returned with a vengeance the following autumn. In his final campaign with the Sooners, he carried the ball 167 times for 1,072 yards and 18 touchdowns, which included a 195-yard effort against Notre Dame.

That game put Vessels on the national radar, and three weeks later he became OU's first Heisman Trophy winner.

"I didn't get the chance to play with Billy Vessels, but I played against him when he came back for an alumni game after his senior season. I went to tackle him once and I found out just how big and strong he really was," said Jimmy Harris, who played quarterback and defensive back from 1954-56. "He was the best OU player I ever saw—smart and tough. He could do it all."

The Statement

George L. Cross was bright, innovative and a born leader, qualities that made him a great success during his 25 years as University of Oklahoma president. He was also a good judge of character.

Cross was responsible for bringing in a young assistant coach named Bud Wilkinson after World War II. Almost 20 years later, he hired Jim Mackenzie, who had a young assistant coach on his staff named Barry Switzer. It was no coincidence Cross was a major factor in the Sooners' rise to greatness both as a football program and a university.

"Originally, Dr. Cross set out to build a football program the state of Oklahoma could be proud of because of an existing inferiority complex that stemmed from the whole *Grapes of Wrath* image they had here at the time," said Switzer. "He felt like a great football team would bring the university attention and give the people something to rally around."

With the OU football program entrenched in the national spotlight, Cross set out to balance the academic side of things.

During an early 1950s budget presentation to the Oklahoma State Legislature, Cross was asked why he needed so much more funding for his university. His facetious, yet honest reply became legend within Sooner circles:

"I would like to build a university of which the football team could be proud."

Indeed.

1950, the First Title

An eighth-year senior named Claude was the quarterback, and his supporting cast was a mixture of mostly sophomores and first-time starters. Many of the players who had returned after the war was over were gone, leaving coach Bud Wilkinson to sort through a roster of names and faces he barely recognized.

How could Oklahoma ever expect to compete for the national title?

For some odd reason, it worked, and the Sooners were contenders.

Claude Arnold, who had initially gone to OU in 1942 prior to going into the service, proved to be a savvy leader. His work under center and the running of backs like Billy Vessels and Leon "Mule Train" Heath made the Sooner offense nearly unstoppable.

They finished off a perfect regular season with a 41-14 romp against Oklahoma A&M and were voted national champions a few days later.

Right-Hand Man

Gomer Jones is a name synonymous with the Bud Wilkinson era. After joining Wilkinson's staff in 1947, the former Nebraska assistant became an important figure in the success of OU's program.

Jones' background was as a line coach, but his teaching abilities encompassed all aspects of the offense, including the quarterback position. He served as Wilkinson's sounding board, and the two would finalize their game plan during a stroll around the field prior to every game.

The two men were close friends on the field and off. Their relationship developed over time and went far beyond football. They shared more than just the sidelines at Memorial Stadium; they shared a mutual respect.

Part of Jones' job was to maintain relations with the players. He listened to problems, administered discipline and made sure everything was running smoothly on and off the field.

Quarterback Jimmy Harris remembers Jones for his ability as a coach and a mentor.

"Gomer was very different than Coach Wilkinson. He had to be more vocal and more animated in certain situations," said Harris. "We got to know Gomer so much better than anyone else on the team because he worked with the quarterbacks. He was just a good coach and a good man.

"He looked up to Coach Wilkinson and I know he had [Bud's] respect."

Keeping the Streak Alive

Bud Wilkinson was never one to give emotional halftime pep talks or "Win one for the Gipper" speeches. Of course, his Sooners rarely trailed during intermissions, so the opportunity didn't present itself too often.

The exception came during the 1956 Colorado game in Boulder. The Sooners, fresh off of a 40-0 romp over Notre Dame, turned in an uninspired first-half performance against the Buffs' single-wing attack. The result was a 19-6 deficit that obviously did not sit well with Wilkinson in the midst of his team's 47-game winning streak.

The soft-spoken coach addressed his players in the locker room, starting with the startlingly loud comment, "You guys don't deserve to wear those red jerseys on your backs." That was enough to get every man's undivided attention.

Wilkinson reminded his team of all the players who had come before and all of the sacrifices they had made.

"Coach Wilkinson had a way of getting his people back to the business at hand, whether it was in practice or at a game," said running back Clendon Thomas. "We knew exactly what he was talking about when he mentioned the red jerseys. Someone wrote in a book once that he asked us to take off the jerseys that day, but that never happened."

The only dramatic event that took place after Wilkinson's speech occurred on the field where the Sooners went back out and dismantled Colorado in the second half.

"We knew we had the better talent and I honestly wasn't worried about our chances to come back and win," said quarterback Jimmy Harris. "Coach Wilkinson got his point across, and that was all that needed to be said."

Final score: OU 27, CU 19. Thirty-six straight.

All Work, Then Play

Perfection was Bud Wilkinson's trump card. He demanded it from himself and from his players. And Oklahoma's trip to the 1959 Orange Bowl is the perfect example.

While some teams looked at a bowl trip as a reward for a successful season, allowing their players to relax and soak up the atmosphere, Wilkinson had a different view. Even though the Sooners' hopes for a national title had faded with a 15-14 loss to Texas, he was all business.

From the moment the Sooners arrived in Miami the week before their game against Syracuse, they were working to improve and polish Wilkinson's game plan. Long two-a-day practices left little time for any sight-seeing tours or trips to the beach.

Wilkinson was interested in only one thing—winning.

"I remember when we landed and arrived at the hotel, Coach Wilkinson got us in the lobby and told us our shoes, shorts and T-shirts were already laid out for us on our beds," said center Bob Harris. "He said get them on and get back down here."

When the players returned to the lobby, Wilkinson marched them out into the streets of Miami and had them run for almost two hours.

The Sooners' regular schedule starting the next day was: up at 5:30 a.m., bus across town to the practice facility, work out for two to three hours, stop briefly for lunch and then hit it again for two more hours.

"You barely had time to find some shade and eat a couple of sandwiches," said Harris. "And by the time we drove back to the hotel and ate dinner, we were so exhausted we didn't have the energy to go anywhere. It was no picnic."

Wilkinson's rigorous schedule lasted for five days, and on Friday, with the game only 24 hours away, he only worked the team out once.

A big performance from Prentice Gautt, whose 42-yard scoring run on the game's second play gave OU a lead it would not relinquish, and the Sooners went on to beat Syracuse 21-7. Afterward, Wilkinson rewarded his team by staying in Miami for two more days.

Eight Points Away

Oklahoma won three national championships under the tutelage of Bud Wilkinson during the 1950s. Amazingly, the Sooners could have won three more titles—in 1954, '57 and '58—if circumstances would have been altered just slightly.

Wilkinson's crew, despite posting a perfect 10-0 record, finished third behind Ohio State and UCLA in '54. Then after earning back-to-back national crowns, a 7-0 loss to Notre Dame cost OU a chance at three straight and also snapped the longest winning streak in history at 47 games.

The following season, a heartbreaking 15-14 loss to arch-rival Texas was the lone blemish on the Sooners' slate. The Longhorns, who trailed 14-8 late, scored on a pass play in the closing seconds and kicked the extra point to seal the win. That was enough to end any thoughts of a national title.

"We were disappointed we didn't win it in 1954, but maybe we weren't as impressive as some of the other teams," said OU quarterback Jimmy Harris. "The eastern press in Chicago and New York was so dominating. They obviously knew about Oklahoma because we had been good for a while, but it seemed we didn't get the same attention at times."

Brothers in Arms

When George Farmer, Charles Parker, Sylvester Norwood of Dunjee High School, and Frank Wilson Jr. of Oklahoma City Douglass, checked out practice gear on September 12, 1955, they were not looking to make any headlines. But since they were the first African-American players to try out in the 61-year history of the OU football program, their presence did not go unnoticed.

And while none of the four were successful in their bids to become the first players of their race to make the OU roster, they helped open the door for future generations of black players, such as the legendary Prentice Gautt.

Bronco's Story

The depth charts for some of Bud Wilkinson's OU teams were filled with positions that listed as many as a dozen names from top to bottom. Plenty of good football players never saw the field during the season because they were buried behind too many guys with more talent.

Bronco McGugan was a victim of the number games. A smallish 152-pound center, he refused to quit despite taking some serious beatings during Wilkinson's rigorous practice sessions. McGugan was so far down on the depth chart, he was not even issued a regular helmet. Instead, he wore an old leather one left over from a decade earlier.

McGugan, however, had a cult following, of sorts. His name drew attention and he eventually became known as the All-American Sub. Sooner fans formed the McGugan Marching and Chowder Society and raised money to purchase a new white helmet like his teammates wore.

His popularity grew to the point that *Time Magazine* did a story on McGugan.

Bud vs. Jim

It was a matchup of monumental proportion—a classic student vs. mentor showdown that had the entire Sooner nation on edge.

Bud Wilkinson's OU squad ran roughshod over its conference rivals in 1953, and in the process set up an Orange Bowl battle with top-ranked Maryland. The Terrapins were coached by the same Jim Tatum who led the Sooners to an 8-3 mark seven seasons earlier. Tatum was also responsible, in part, for bringing Wilkinson to OU.

Three weeks before the much-anticipated game, Maryland was crowned national champion, and a week prior to that, Tatum returned to Norman to scout the Sooners.

Tatum bragged on his Terps and believed they would finish off a perfect season against his former team. But Wilkinson and company had other ideas. OU's defense played brilliantly and the offense squeezed just enough juice out of its running game to produce the game's only touchdown—a Larry Grigg run by way of a J. D. Roberts path-clearing block.

The Sooners earned a hard-fought 7-0 victory. And in the aftermath, Tatum confessed that Wilkinson had outcoached him.

End of the Streak

After a close call with Colorado (14-13) on October 26, 1957, Oklahoma had beaten Kansas State and Missouri to stretch college football's longest winning streak to 47 straight games. An unranked Notre Dame team came to Norman trying to avenge a 40-0 thrashing the season before, but without much firepower to back its mission.

But as luck of the Irish would have it, a flu epidemic had been raging on campus, and several dozen of Bud Wilkinson's players were still trying to recover when Saturday rolled around.

"There were a lot of guys who had been sick, but we never used that as an excuse," said center Bob Harris. "We should have defeated Notre Dame that day."

It had been four years since the Sooners had tasted defeat, but a struggling offense put the streak in jeopardy from the opening quarter. Notre Dame's defense would not budge, and the game entered the fourth quarter still scoreless.

Wilkinson could almost see the writing on the wall.

"I was willing to settle for a scoreless tie in the third quarter," he commented.

The Irish were in no mood for a tie. Quarterback Bob Williams directed a 20-play, 80-yard drive that culminated with a Dick Lynch scoring run with 3:50 remaining. But trailing 7-0, Oklahoma fans still believed the Sooners would find a way to win.

Williams made sure that didn't happen. After the Sooners had marched inside the Irish 10-yard line, the Notre Dame senior intercepted a pass with under a minute to go. Almost 62,000 OU fans sat stunned as the clock expired.

"We were disappointed. That was only natural, but it wasn't like it was the end of the world," said running back Jakie Sandefer. "I remember Coach Wilkinson coming into the dressing room and saying, 'I'm proud of you guys. You've been part of winning 47 straight games. That is something no major college team will ever do again. Just remember, the only men who never lose are the men that never play.'"

Perfect Quarterback

When Bud Wilkinson brought in Terrell, Texas, halfback Jimmy Harris in 1953, he spent all of a week running plays with the backs. OU's coach had other ideas for Harris, and he began executing those plans by moving the speedy freshman to quarterback.

Harris was sixth on the depth chart when he made the switch.

"Coach Wilkinson said he might try me at quarterback before I signed. And I didn't really care—I just wanted to play at Oklahoma," said Harris.

Wilkinson was impressed with Harris' leadership qualities and he noticed the young man had extremely quick hands and good instincts. He was already a fearless defensive halfback, and he was athletic enough to make the transition to QB look easy.

Deep inside, Wilkinson believed Harris might just be the future of his program.

When Harris took over the job during his sophomore season in 1954, it didn't take him long to prove his coach right. Oklahoma finished 10-0 with Harris at the helm that fall and followed that up with back-to-back national championship seasons.

"I was fortunate to play at OU at a time when the surrounding talent was just so deep," said Harris, who was 25-0 as the Sooners' starting quarterback. "We had the best coach and the best players in the country. That made my job a lot easier.

"At the time, I didn't think anything of the winning streak. I felt like I was supposed to win them all."

A Brush with Greatness

After playing the entire 1947 season with two bad elbows and a banged-up shoulder, Merle Dinkins finally agreed to a medical examination. Doctors determined both of his elbows needed reconstructive surgery, and they opted to operate on both at the same time.

Recovering in his hospital bed afterward, Dinkins was helpless to do anything that required using his arms. So when teammate Stan West dropped by for a visit, Dinkins decided to make the most of the situation and asked West if he would brush his teeth.

West thought for a moment and answered, "I'll do it, Merle, but that's as far as this friendship goes."

Team Unity

Although there were players who did not like the fact Bud Wilkinson brought in an African-American running back to play for Oklahoma in 1956, Prentice Gautt said he was greeted with encouragement and consideration from many of his new teammates and coaches. But that did not mean there would not be plenty of other hurdles to overcome, as many parts of the country resisted integration at any level of society.

While Gautt often was not allowed to stay in the same hotel as his teammates or eat at the same restaurants, a certain display of unity one evening provided more than a little hope.

OU's freshman team had just played Tulsa and then stopped at a local eatery on the way back to Norman. But upon seeing Gautt, the manager told him they did not serve Negroes and asked him to go to the basement to eat his meal.

"I told him I had played with the guys, and if I couldn't eat with them, I wouldn't eat at all," said Gautt, who retreated to the team bus in tears.

After watching the event unfold, Gautt's teammates began a mass exodus to the parking lot as a show of support.

"Port [Robertson] had already gone out to console Prentice, but we weren't going to sit there and eat without him," said teammate Brewster Hobby. "Getting up and leaving was the right thing to do. Prentice was a part of our team, and what they did wasn't right."

The show of support boosted Gautt's spirits and helped further bond him with his teammates.

Platoon System

Bud Wilkinson believed since most of his players went both ways, meaning they were on the field for long periods of time during games, that a platoon system would help keep his squad fresh for the fourth quarter. Wilkinson always said that's when games were won or lost.

So the OU coach had a first unit and a second unit that shared playing time every game.

Doc Hearon, a member of the second unit, wanted to be a starter, and he went to assistant coach Gomer Jones to voice his opinion one day.

"Coach, I ought to be on first string," he said, to which Jones replied, "Doc, we don't have a first string. We've got two teams and it's all equal."

Hearon looked at Jones for a moment and said, "If that's the case, then I'd like to be on that other team."

Roomies

The top-ranked Sooners opened up the 1957 season on the road at No. 8 Pittsburgh. It was the first varsity season for OU's first African-American player, Prentice Gautt, who had earned the number-two spot on the depth chart at running back behind Jakie Sandefer.

On road trips, the top two players on the depth chart at each position shared a room. But when the list was handed out in the hotel lobby upon the team's arrival, Sandefer was listed with third-teamer Bobby Boyd.

"I went to Coach Wilkinson and told him I had no problems rooming with Prentice, but he said that had nothing to do with it. He explained that Prentice had fumbled a couple of times in the last practice and that's why he had been moved to third team," explained Sandefer.

The next week, Wilkinson called Sandefer in for a meeting and asked if he would mind rooming with Gautt on the remainder of the team's road trips. Sandefer agreed.

Even after Gautt was moved to fullback the following season, the two men remained roommates on the road.

"We did that for two seasons and became good friends," said Sandefer. "Prentice was a prince of a guy. Was he different? Yeah, he was different—mostly because he was a better student and a better person than most of the guys on the team. He was special."

Tough Love

No person in the University of Oklahoma athletics department was more respected or feared than Port Robertson. He served as head wrestling coach, conditioning coach and academic advisor during a career that spanned 40 years from 1947-86.

Besides producing consistent winners on the mat—his teams won three national titles during a 14-year period—Robertson ruled with an iron fist when it came to academia.

Miss a class, answer to Port. Skip study hall, answer to Port.

Robertson was responsible for helping more than a few student athletes find their way to graduation during his time at OU. One of the football players who benefited from Robertson's tough love methods was Jerry Pettibone.

Pettibone was sleep walking through his freshman season at OU, buried on the depth chart and uninspired by school. He was teetering on the brink of becoming an academic casualty when Robertson stepped in with a phone call to Pettibone's father.

By the time their conversation ended, the younger Pettibone was an unknowing member of Robertson's straight and narrow "peahead" club.

"Port calls me into his office one day and just starts reading me the riot act about my school work," said Pettibone. "He tells me what I'm going to do to improve and flourish at OU and every time he made a point he'd jab his finger into my sternum. That got my attention in a hurry."

But Pettibone was going to have nothing to do with Robertson's hard-core rules. He immediately phoned his father and began describing how Robertson yelled at him and threatened him and even got physical with him. Pettibone told his father he was going to find a better school and transfer.

When the younger Pettibone was finished describing his ordeal, father Pettibone told him to get used to Robertson's ways and forget about transferring.

"Basically, he said it was time to step up and be responsible for my actions," added Pettibone, who went on to letter in football and graduate in four years. "After a while, I understood what Port was doing, and I came to appreciate him like a lot of other athletes over the years."

Pettibone later returned to serve as an assistant football coach at OU. Many days he worked side by side with Robertson.

Almost First Team

There were many good football players during the Bud Wilkinson era who never quite broke into the lineup or found the spotlight. Wray Littlejohn was one of those men.

"No one tried harder than Wray Littlejohn. He worked so hard. But he just wasn't quite at the same level as some of the guys in front of him," said Norman McNabb, who served as an assistant coach to Wilkinson. "I'm sure it was frustrating for him at times."

Littlejohn was known to say, many times, "I'd be first team Monday through Thursday and then they'd put a damn Burris brother in front of me."

Between 1946 and 1956, four Burris brothers—Buddy, Kurt, Bob and Lynn—played for the Sooners.

Back-to-Back Titles

Oklahoma had experienced the national stage in 1950 when it earned its first national championship in football. But celebration had been tempered thanks to a 13-7 loss to Kentucky in the Sugar Bowl weeks later.

There was no second-guessing and very few doubters in 1955 and 1956. Both of those OU teams were incredible. Bud

Wilkinson had built a talented machine that oozed confidence and took no prisoners.

After failing to win the national title despite a 10-0 mark in 1954, the Sooners were not about to settle for anything less than ultimate perfection during the two ensuing seasons.

Led by marquee players like Tommy McDonald, Ed Gray, Jerry Tubbs and Clendon Thomas, the Sooners were unstoppable. They posted 11 shutouts in those two seasons and topped the 40-point mark offensively 13 times.

OU dominated the college football world like few teams had ever done.

Wahoo McDaniel

"Ornery. He had more fun off the field and on it."

That's how many of Ed "Wahoo" McDaniel's Oklahoma teammates described him during his stint as a linebacker for the Sooners from 1957-59. An imposing 250 pounds, McDaniel possessed many talents on the football field and displayed a zest for life away from the game.

McDaniel made the transition from schoolboy star to collegiate standout for coach Bud Wilkinson's OU program, and he still owns the record for the longest punt in school history—a 91-yarder against Iowa State in 1958. On top of that, his 86-yard touchdown reception from Bobby Boyd still ranks as the fifth longest pass play.

Off the field, McDaniel once ran 36 miles from Norman to Chickasha as part of a $50 bet between members of the football team and campus fraternity. Running against a makeshift relay team that included two members of OU's track team, McDaniel led the first 31 miles before running out of gas and stopping short of his final destination.

McDaniel's success with the Sooners did not compare with the stardom he achieved during and after an eight-year career in the AFL, when he crossed over to professional wrestling. During his 30 years as a wrestler, McDaniel transformed himself into one of the most popular and admired figures in the sport.

14 Straight Conference Titles

Winning 47 straight games is nothing short of spectacular. It's a record that has stood the test of time and one many people believe will never be approached.

But Oklahoma's football teams produced a few other impressive streaks during the late 1940s and into the '50s. The one that shines brightest is the fact that the Sooners won 14 straight conference titles.

From 1946, Jim Tatum's lone season as head coach, to 1959, OU captured its conference's crown every single season. Not only did Bud Wilkinson's program string together all of those titles, it did not lose to any conference foe from 1947-59.

Lucky Suit

There were many elements that factored into Oklahoma's legendary 47-game winning streak, including clutch performances, great determination and a few lucky bounces. There was also "The Suit."

Bud Wilkinson was known to be superstitious, and when he found something that worked, he stuck with it, especially when it came to his football program. One thing that seemed to work for the duration of OU's famous streak was Wilkinson's clothes. For each of the 47 games, Wilkinson wore the same gray suit, white shirt, red tie, gray socks and hat.

Hard to Swallow

Smokey Holland was almost 25 years old when he returned home from the Korean War in 1953. He was the elder statesman as far as the freshman class was concerned, and he acted a little more worldly.

That wasn't necessarily a good thing.

During one of the first fall practices, Holland was stretching and going through workouts when he was approached by freshman coach Port Robertson.

"Mr. Holland, I know that you are older and a lot wiser than the young kids on this team, but if that's tobacco in your mouth, you need to do that on your own time," offered Robertson.

Point taken. "OK, Coach, I'll spit it out and won't do it any more."

A couple of days later, Holland was working out during practice and Robertson noticed a little sag in his lip.

"Mr. Holland, is that tobacco in your mouth?" he asked.

"Yes, Coach," Holland answered.

But before he could even finish the short answer, Robertson had wrestled him to the ground and made him swallow the tobacco. Holland turned about five shades of green and never once returned to practice with tobacco in his mouth the rest of the season.

Coaching Schools

In the years after Bud Wilkinson established Oklahoma as a national power on the college football scene, high school, college and even professional coaches from around the country wanted to know the secret to Wilkinson's success. To accommodate all of the letters, telegrams and phone calls, the Sooner coach began hosting a coaching school during the off-season.

Wilkinson would demonstrate his system and break down the various elements he believed were critical to the success of his OU program. Coaches came from everywhere to listen to the Great White Father talk football.

During the decade of the 1950s, Wilkinson earned more money conducting class in his school than he ever dreamed of making as the coach at Oklahoma.

Sabotaged or Bad Luck?

When Oklahoma traveled to Chicago for its 1959 season opener with Northwestern, little did it know opposition much more powerful than the Wildcats was lurking in the shadows.

Bud Wilkinson's Sooners were ranked second in the country, and Northwestern was given little chance to win the contest.

As was customary for Wilkinson-coached teams, the Sooners arrived three days early to begin final preparations. On Wednesday night, the team had reservations at the Chez Paris dinner club. It was a time to eat, relax and enjoy before getting down to business the following day.

Late in the meal, a handful of players began to show signs of illness. And it was getting worse by the minute. As many as eight Sooners were taken by taxi to a local hospital, supposedly suffering from some kind of food poisoning.

The team was in total shock. Team officials began looking for answers and hoping the sick players were going to be OK by Saturday. Of course, by the time they turned their investigation back to the restaurant, the evidence was long gone.

It was believed that a drug such as morphine was placed in the jello, and rumors began circulating that several big Chicago gamblers were responsible.

"We ate everything in sight that night," said guard Karl Milstead. "The only thing I didn't eat was the jello. So I always figured that must have been it."

Milstead said the players heard talk of a police investigation, but that nothing ever came of it.

Meanwhile, the eight sick players spent most of the next two days in the hospital. They were released in time for Friday practice, but were in no shape to help the team at that point.

"Those guys were all weak and still recovering by the time the game rolled around," added Milstead. "We just weren't the same team, especially without [quarterback] Bobby Boyd. "We got the hell beat out of us that day."

To worsen matters for the Sooners, a huge thunderstorm hovered over the stadium that day. Northwestern took the lead early and rolled to a 45-13 victory.

Royal Treatment

Darrell Royal was a disciple of Bud Wilkinson. He played for the man, respected him and loved him.

And when Royal got the head coaching job at Texas in 1956, he learned to beat his idol, over and over. In fact, during Wilkinson's final six seasons at Oklahoma, his Sooners lost six times to Royal's Longhorns.

To that point in his career, Wilkinson had owned a 9-2 record versus Texas.

I'll Take that Bet

Breckenridge, Texas, native Larry Munnerlyn was a character to the core. A backup tackle most of his playing career at OU, Munnerlyn entertained his teammates with wild stories and even wilder acts.

He would take a $2 bet just for the fun of it. No matter how crazy or outlandish the bet.

During the 1958 off season, several Sooner players were discussing the frozen condition one night of the reflection pool located just outside the window of the study hall they were in. Munnerlyn joined the conversation, and one of his teammates said he would give a $1 to anyone brave enough to crack the ice on the pool and take a swim.

Munnerlyn could not resist. And he survived to tell about it.

"Larry earned the reputation of being a little on the crazy side, but he was a really good fella," said teammate Brewster Hobby.

One time, Munnerlyn allegedly drank an entire quart of motor oil as a result of a $1 wager.

CHAPTER FOUR

The 1960s

"58 Special"

BUD WILKINSON'S OU PLAYBOOK rarely relied on gimmicks or trickery, although the occasional sleight of hand did make its way into the Sooners' split-T attack. Such was the case during the 1962 season, and it came from a pair of unlikely sources.

Early on, the Sooners were having problems getting their offense jump-started. A 7-3 win over Syracuse in the season opener was followed by a 13-7 home loss to Notre Dame. Moving the ball was a problem, and Wilkinson was searching for answers.

The Sooners had a week off before traveling to Dallas to meet Texas. One day after practice, Wilkinson spotted third-team quarterback Ronnie Fletcher throwing long passes to a scout team freshman named Lance Rentzel. Intrigued by the aerial display, Wilkinson invited Fletcher and Rentzel to his office the following day. He explained to the pair that he might be interested in putting their skills to use in a future game.

Wilkinson designed a halfback pass play called "58 Special" and had Fletcher and Rentzel work on it that week. Neither player figured the coach would call the play, especially when they learned that Fletcher would be riding the team bus to

Dallas while Rentzel would have to provide his own transportation.

"They packed Lance's gear on the bus, but he had to drive his '57 Thunderbird and meet us in Dallas the next day," said Fletcher. "We never thought we'd actually get into the game."

Their chances of hooking up were further jeopardized when Rentzel's car broke down near Marietta, Oklahoma. Although he managed to hitch a ride, Rentzel did not arrive until late Friday evening. Two hours prior to kickoff, he made it to the OU locker room at the Cotton Bowl.

As it turned out, the Sooners' offensive struggles continued that day and they found themselves trailing the Longhorns 9-0 with 40 seconds left in the opening half. That's when Wilkinson decided to unveil "58 Special." Quarterback Norman Smith took the snap and pitched the ball to Fletcher, who rolled right and fired a 40-yard pass to Rentzel, who was tackled at the Texas 40.

As the pair started back to the sideline, Wilkinson motioned them to stay. He called the same play to the opposite side. This time, Rentzel outmaneuvered UT defender Jimmy Hudson and hauled in Fletcher's pass for an Oklahoma touchdown.

Figuring Texas would not fall for the play again, Wilkinson did not call on the services of Fletcher and Rentzel again that afternoon. The Sooners eventually lost 9-6.

Who's the New Guy?

Bud Wilkinson was in for a surprise during his team's annual picture day prior to the 1962 season. Upon his arrival at the photo session at Owen Field, the legendary coach spotted an imposing-looking lad ripped with muscles whom he did not recognize.

After checking with his staff, Wilkinson discovered the player was a little-known recruit from Cameron College in

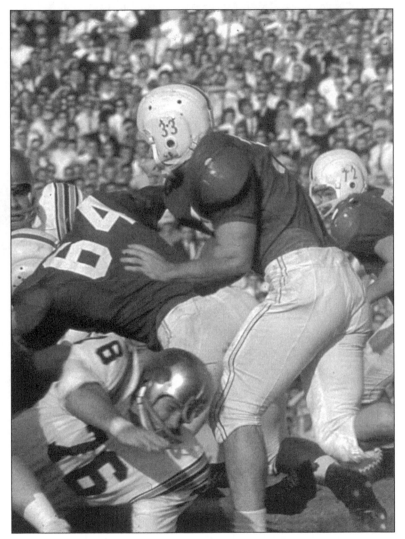

No. 33 Joe Don Looney. *Photo courtesy of the University of Oklahoma*

Lawton, Oklahoma. His name was Joe Don Looney, and he did not remain a little-known recruit for long.

In the Sooners' opening game that season, Looney began to cultivate his legend as both a fine football player and unmanageable revolutionary.

Looney made his debut with OU trailing Syracuse 3-0, and upon entering the huddle late in the contest, told quarterback Monte Deere, "Give me the damn ball, I'm going for a touchdown." The first time the rookie back touched the ball, he sprinted 60 yards for the only TD of the game.

OU won 7-3, and Looney's closing heroics made national headlines.

A Visit from Jack

An hour before Oklahoma was scheduled to do battle with Bear Bryant's Alabama squad in the 1963 Orange Bowl, Bud Wilkinson's Sooners got a locker-room visit from President John F. Kennedy.

Kennedy had developed a working relationship with Wilkinson after the coach signed on to direct his national fitness program a year earlier. Wilkinson began the visit by saying "Fellas, there's a friend of mine I'd like you to meet..."

While talking about the fitness program, Kennedy walked up to OU player Larry Vermillion and gave him a playful punch in his oversized belly. Looking up at Wilkinson, the president said, "Is he all right?"

The looming tension in the room gave way to laughter.

End of the Road

An award-winning author, Harold Keith became the uttermost authority on Oklahoma athletics, especially football, during a 39-year stint as the school's sports information director. Hired by OU athletic director Bennie Owen in 1930, Keith became a fixture at his alma mater.

His job was to record and dispense information relating to OU sporting events, but Keith did much more. His sense of history and articulate nature were legendary. He wrote 16 books and served as president of the College Sports Information

Directors of America, earning that organization's famed Arch Ward Award in 1961.

In his book *Forty-Seven Straight!*, Keith chronicled the Sooners' record winning streak during the mid-1950s, at all of which he had a front-row seat.

"Harold was the ultimate authority, but he never acted like it. He was one of the first people to do sports information as a profession. For years, he lived what people consider history today," said Mike Prusinski, OU sports information director from 1988-2000. "He could tell stories that you'd be happy to sit around and listen to for hours, taking in every single word. He was special."

Keith retired on July 1, 1969, and was succeeded by his son, John.

Sooner Dreams

Growing up in Miami, Oklahoma, Steve Owens was fated to become a University of Oklahoma football fan. As a young boy, he dreamed of playing for the Sooners and becoming part of the tradition Bud Wilkinson continued to shape every autumn.

Owens developed into an outstanding athlete and nurtured his love of OU football every chance he got. As a teenager, he worked at a local shoe store called The Hub, and on Saturdays he would more often than not find himself in the storeroom listening to OU games on the radio.

"We didn't sell too many shoes on Saturday afternoons," laughed Owens. "The owner of the store was a big OU fan, too, and we both listened to the games as much as possible."

As Owens matured into one of the top running backs in the state, his recruiting stock shot off the scale with many of the major college programs in the country. Unfortunately, OU had fallen on hard times during his senior season at Miami. The Sooners finished 3-7 that fall under Gomer Jones, and he resigned shortly thereafter.

"I had a chance to go to a lot of different schools, but I was mostly looking at Arkansas and Oklahoma," explained Owens. "Arkansas coach Jim Mackenzie was really after me, and I knew it was going to be a tough decision."

Then fate stepped in. Oklahoma hired Mackenzie to replace Jones, and his first phone call was to Owens.

"He said forget everything I told you about Arkansas. You've always wanted to go to Oklahoma and that's where you need to go," laughed Owens.

By the time he was through in Norman, Owens had rewritten almost every OU rushing record, including career touchdowns (56) and career yards (3,867). He also became the first Sooner since Billy Vessels in 1952 to win the Heisman Trophy.

The Wicked Worm

Bobby Warmack was never one to seek publicity or try to draw attention to himself during his quarterbacking days at Oklahoma in the mid-1960s. In fact, he was more than happy to quietly go about his duties under center and let the spotlight fall on any of his surrounding cast, namely running back Steve Owens.

Charged by coaches Jim Mackenzie and Chuck Fairbanks, Warmack helped lead a revival of OU football during his time as starting quarterback. After finishing 6-4 in 1966 with victories over Texas and Big Eight champion Nebraska, the Sooners turned the following season into a magical journey that saw them go 10-1 and win the Orange Bowl.

It wasn't until just before that season-capping win over Tennessee, 26-24, that Warmack started receiving his due. While prepping to play in the Orange Bowl, OU players noticed Vols standout quarterback Dewey Warren was affectionately called the "Swamp Rat" by his teammates and fans. So they decided to come up with a clever nickname for their quarterback.

"Gene Cagle tagged me the 'Wicked Worm.' I guess it had something to do with my running ability. I kind of slithered here and slithered there, nothing too fancy," said Warmack.

The nickname may not have struck fear into the hearts of opposing defenses, but Warmack was a winner. He went 21-9 as a starter during his Sooner career and has been described as one of the most underrated quarterbacks in Sooner history.

Hey, Heppy

Harry Daniel Hettmannsperger Jr. That's more than a mouthful. And Hettmannsperger was more than just a college football player. He was a unique character who marched to the beat of a different drum in 1966.

"Heppy," as he was called by teammates, often found himself in Chuck Fairbanks' doghouse. He was the OU Police Department's worst nightmare, always doing something foolish to draw its ire.

"Heppy was quite a character, very unique," said teammate Steve Owens. "He was a very strong individual and a heckuva linebacker."

Hettmannsperger used to demonstrate his strength by taking rope-climbing wagers during OU's fourth-quarter workouts on the south base. While everyone else was struggling to get up a 30-foot rope the conventional way, Hettmannsperger bet teammates he could do it upside down.

"You didn't want to bet against Heppy when it came to something like that. He was amazing when it came to things like that," added Owens.

Unfortunately for Hettmannsperger, while there were innocent stunts like being able to pick his nose with his tongue, he couldn't stay out of trouble with the local authorities.

One night, Hettmannsperger was speeding around campus when the OU police began chasing him. By the time they finally cornered him on the south oval, there were 10 police cars and 20 officers involved. It took just about all 20 to restrain the

OU starter, who threw several of the officers over his car before being subdued.

Blank Check

Lance Rentzel parked wherever he wanted to park on campus. Restricted lots meant nothing to the flamboyant running back and his 1957 Thunderbird.

During the course of his four-year stint with the OU football team, Rentzel racked up dozens of parking tickets that he basically ignored, at least until his senior year. That's when he took the tickets and a blank check to the OU Campus Police Department.

"It's signed," Rentzel said.

"Just fill out the amount and cash it when I graduate."

Problem Child

Members of Bud Wilkinson's coaching staff were amazed with what running back Joe Don Looney could do on a football field. He was fast, strong, agile and instinctive.

It was the way Looney carried himself off the field that worried Wilkinson and company.

During a coaches' meeting shortly after Looney's arrival to Norman, one of the assistant coaches expressed his concern:

"If we are going to keep this guy on our team, we're going to have to hire a psychologist. We can't control him by ourselves."

Sign, Then Sit

In the aftermath of an exciting Bedlam victory over Oklahoma State that concluded the 1964 regular season, four Oklahoma players were approached by and eventually signed with an agent looking to represent them during their professional playing careers. Since it was a violation of NCAA rules to sign with an agent before the end of the season, the players were sworn to secrecy until the Sooners finished off the campaign at the '65 Gator Bowl.

But on the eve of the January 2 game with Florida State, the news broke that Lance Rentzel, Ralph Neely, Jim Grisham and Wes Skidgel were being suspended due to their dealings with an agent. The team was informed by head coach Gomer Jones during a team meeting less than 24 hours prior to kickoff.

The following day, still in shock, the Sooners were burned for four touchdown passes by receiver Fred Biletnikoff, who finished the 36-19 FSU victory with 13 catches for 192 yards.

Hey, We Care

The 1969 season would not be all that memorable for OU football fans if not for the extraordinary performance of Steve Owens. Inconsistent defense had the Sooners headed for a 6-4 mark, despite the fact Owens was churning up yardage and scoring touchdowns at record pace.

OU's heralded back was running his way toward the Heisman Trophy, and his numbers grew more impressive by the week. He entered the Colorado game having rushed for 100-plus yards in 13 straight games, and no one figured the Buffs would put an end to that.

But the Sooners scored early and often without a whole lot of help from Owens, who had totaled a little over 80 yards by mid-fourth quarter. With OU leading 35-23 and the final minutes winding down, Owens told quarterback Jack Mildren to simply kneel on the ball and end the game.

"That didn't go over too big," said Owens. "I said [the 100 yards] didn't matter to me as long as we were winning. Well, one of our guards, Billy Elfstrom, looked over at me and said, 'It might not matter to you, but it matters to us.'"

Elfstrom was, of course, talking about the offensive line unit that had been opening holes for Owens for three seasons.

Well, Owens got the ball three more times and kept his 100-yard-game streak alive, which eventually ended at 18.

Remembering the Land Run

Although it would not become the official mascot until the October 6, 1980 season, the Sooner Schooner became a popular addition to Oklahoma's rich football tradition 19 years earlier when the Bartlett Foundation began donating it for Saturday games. The Bartlett family had originally built the Conestoga with hopes that the covered wagon replica similar to those used by the pioneers who settled in Oklahoma would eventually be phased in as official mascot.

Powered by matching white Shetland ponies, originally named "Mike" and "Ike" after the popular candy, the Sooner Schooner represented the essence of the infamous 1889 Oklahoma Land Run. These days, the Schooner is pulled by "Boomer" and "Sooner" across Owen Field after every Sooner score, and it has become one of the most recognized symbols of OU athletics.

The Sooner Schooner. *Photo courtesy of the University of Oklahoma*

The Schooner, which is driven by members of the Oklahoma RUF/NEKS spirit group, is still maintained and quartered at the Bartlett Ranch in Sapulpa, Oklahoma.

Now Boarding

Jim Mackenzie almost never became head football coach at Oklahoma. And it had nothing to do with his strategy, vision or ability on the sidelines. He was well equipped in all of those categories, and he was more than qualified to lead what many believed was the necessary revival of the Sooner program.

It also had little to do with the fact the Sooner braintrust was trying to persuade Texas coach Darrell Royal to return to his alma mater. Instead, it was a short nap that nearly cost Mackenzie his chance in Norman.

After completing the 1965 season as the top assistant on Frank Broyles' Arkansas staff, Mackenzie was contacted, with much difficulty, about possibly replacing the retiring Gomer Jones at OU. He scheduled an interview and arranged for a trip to meet OU President George L. Cross.

On his AAR flight from Fayetteville to Oklahoma City, Mackenzie fell asleep and did not wake up when his plane touched down at his intended destination, some 20 miles north of Norman. It wasn't until the plane landed again in Wichita Falls, Texas, an hour later that Mackenzie discovered he had missed OKC.

"He was honestly concerned that missing that interview would cost him any chance at the job. Hell, I would have been worried, too," said Barry Switzer, who was also an assistant at Arkansas at the time. "But he called Dr. Cross and explained the situation, and they rescheduled everything. Fortunately, we were able to laugh about it later."

Ultimately, Mackenzie was hired as OU's head coach in late December 1965. His first move was to surround himself with assistants like Switzer, Chuck Fairbanks, Pat James and Galen Hall.

The File on this Guy

During the final recruiting period of Jim Mackenzie's first season, the Sooners had a couple of extra scholarships they were looking to find good homes for. During the previous fall, Mackenzie had spotted a skinny quarterback at Fort Smith (Arkansas) Southside whom he could not get out of his mind.

"Jim kept saying there was something about this kid. He probably wasn't going to play quarterback, but he might just fill out and make a player," explained assistant coach Barry Switzer. "He thought we should give him a shot."

Mackenzie's instinct turned out to be right. After redshirting as a freshman, Jim Files matured into his 6-foot-3 frame. He became a three-year starter at linebacker for the Sooners and ended up being a number-one draft pick of the New York Giants in 1968. In fact, he was selected six players before teammate and Heisman Trophy winner Steve Owens was by Detroit.

Granny

A decade had passed since Oklahoma had won more than nine games in a single season and truly figured as a legitimate contender for the national title. But the fall of 1967 would prove magical in the resurgence of the Sooners. And a large portion of that magic could be traced to the performance of Granville Liggins.

Liggins was, according to every OU coach on Chuck Fairbanks' staff, the most explosive, most devastating defensive lineman in the country from 1966-67. The physical 5-foot-10, 215-pound Tulsa product was so quick off the ball that OU coaches had to remind game officials to watch the ball and not Granville during snaps.

"That's how quick he was. He was already moving while everyone else was thinking about moving on the snap," said Barry Switzer. "Granville was one of the greatest players to ever

Granville Liggins. *Photo courtesy of the University of Oklahoma*

wear an Oklahoma jersey. No doubt, he was the quickest, most explosive player during my time at OU."

It's been said Liggins defined the nose guard position during his career as a Sooner. His famous charges of opposing centers are still legend in Norman. OU finished 10-1 his senior season, as he earned All-America honors for the second straight year.

And to top off his athletic career at OU, Liggins won the heavyweight title at the 1967 Big Eight Wrestling Championships. In his first and only season on the varsity mat squad, he also earned All-America honors and finished sixth at the NCAA Championships.

The Fourth-Quarter Class

Motivation was not a problem when Jim Mackenzie took over Oklahoma's football program in 1966. He made sure of that in a hurry by implementing a highly rigorous regiment of drills called the fourth-quarter class.

"It was the hardest workout I'd ever been through, or anyone else on the team, for that matter. It was patterned, to some degree, after the things Bear Bryant did in his heyday," said quarterback Bobby Warmack, shaking his head at the very thought of it. "I don't think it was any secret they were trying to set a standard for the type of players they wanted at Oklahoma, and running people off was just part of the process. Those that survived would play."

The dreaded "class" mostly took place in a building at the old South Base near campus and included an array of agility drills, exercises and physical hardships that tested a player's mettle and stamina.

"We did all of that stuff and then we'd go out into the sticker patch and do any number of other drills so that by the time you were through, your sweat top would be full of goatheads and stickers," added Warmack. "It was tough, very tough at times. But they knew what they were doing. I think everyone who went through that and survived was a better man for it."

Stealing from Texas?

Barry Switzer always believed one of the main keys to building a successful football program at Oklahoma was the Sooners' ability to recruit in Texas. The Lone Star State produced an endless pool of talent every year at the high school level, and if OU could just find a way to tap into that pipeline, it would make all the difference in the world.

During the fall of 1967, Switzer found himself hot on the trail of a dandy young quarterback prospect from Abilene, Texas. Jack Mildren was a proven passer whose smarts and leadership ability made him a hot commodity in recruiting circles.

Texas wanted Mildren. Oklahoma wanted him more.

"I was out in Abilene thinking we've really got to sell this kid on what we were doing with our program and how he fits

Barry Switzer. *Photo courtesy of the University of Oklahoma*

in to our future," said Switzer, an assistant for Chuck Fairbanks at the time. "I'm figuring that since he grew up right there in Texas' backyard, I've got to convince him somehow to become a Sooner. But I come to find out that Norman is almost as close to Abilene as Austin is. That's how big Texas is. It's no wonder they produce so many great players down there."

Mildren eventually opted for OU.

"I liked the coaching staff at OU, and the school had everything I wanted," explained Mildren. "I wasn't steeped in OU history, but I knew they had been successful in the past. It was the best situation, and I'll never regret a day of my time there."

Over the next 20 years, many great prep stars from Texas would follow Mildren's path to Norman.

A True All-American

Oklahoma's tradition-rich football program produced its share of heroes over the years, but few more memorable than Bob Kalsu. The strapping offensive tackle was described once by Barry Switzer as "the best offensive lineman on the team," adding, "Bob wasn't only a great player, he was a great leader."

Kalsu proved that during his three-year stint in Norman. Strong, fast and smart, Kalsu earned All-America honors his senior year helping lead Chuck Fairbanks' first OU team to a 10-1 record and an Orange Bowl victory.

Kalsu was drafted in the eighth round by the Buffalo Bills in 1968 and played one season before he was called to join the U.S. Army's 101st Airborne Division in Vietnam. Only 24, Kalsu was killed by North Vietnamese mortar fire on July 21, 1970, thus earning the unfortunate distinction of being the only professional football player to lose his life in that war.

A plaque in his honor at the Pro Football Hall of Fame is inscribed with the following: "No one will ever know how great a football player Bob might have been, but we do know how great a man he was to give up his life to his country."

In 2001, OU coach Bob Stoops established the Bob Kalsu Award, which recognizes uncommon dedication and fortitude. More than 30 years after his death, Kalsu's legacy is stronger than ever.

Light-Hearted Lion

Ask any of the players who donned the crimson and cream at Memorial Stadium during the late 1960s what character they

Bob Kalsu. *Photo courtesy of the University of Oklahoma*

best remember from those days, and almost to a man, they'll bring up the name Byron Bigby.

The South Carolina native was a fun-loving teddy bear when it came to off-the-field antics, but he was a different man every time he dug in in the trenches with OU's offensive line. He was tough. Nicknamed "Big Kid," Bigby was always into some kind of shenanigans when it came to putting smiles on his teammates' faces.

"He kept us in stitches," said All-America tight end Steve Zabel. "He was hysterical. He was a wild man. Byron always managed to put a lighter spin on situations that seemed pretty tough at the time."

From time to time, Bigby experienced difficulty learning all of his blocking assignments in OU's system. When that happened, he would go to the line, get into his four-point stance and look to guard Eddie Lancaster for directions.

"I knew when I saw Byron's head finally settle down into the line, he knew where he was going and I could go ahead and start the snap count," laughed Bobby Warmack, OU's quarterback and Bigby's roommate for a time. "We all still light up every time we see Byron, because he's the one guy who reminds us of who we were and how we were back then."

Gone Too Soon

Oklahoma fans barely had time to embrace Jim Mackenzie, the tough but likeable coach who seemed to have the Sooners pointed in the right direction after one brief season at the helm. The Big Red finished 6-4 during Mackenzie's inaugural season, recording victories over Texas and Nebraska along the way.

The win over the Longhorns was especially sweet since it snapped an eight-game losing streak in Dallas. It was reported that on the day of that victory, Mackenzie smoked five packs of Camel cigarettes.

But before Mackenzie could truly begin enjoying the success he believed was not far away, he died of a heart attack, just 16 months after taking the Oklahoma job. Two months later in May 1967, assistant coach Chuck Fairbanks was named as his replacement.

Barry Switzer once said, "Anybody who knew Jim Mackenzie, loved Jim Mackenzie."

The Black Athlete

While African Americans were making some strides in the equal rights movement as early as the 1950s, it wasn't until the mid-1960s that many of the best black athletes really began to break through the color barriers of most major universities, especially those in the south. Until then, they often attended black colleges due to discrimination and unspoken quotas.

The University of Oklahoma was well ahead of the curve when it came to signing black athletes to scholarships. In 1956, Bud Wilkinson brought in Prentice Gautt, who went on to earn All-Conference honors and help the Sooners forge a 27-5 record during his career.

While the Southwest Conference did not sign a black athlete until 1966—SMU's Jerry LeVias—the Sooners proved more insightful to the north. Players like Ben Hart, Eugene Ross and Granville Liggins were making their mark on OU's history books long before Texas even thought of signing its first black player in 1971.

"It wasn't that Oklahoma was trying to champion any cause; we always just looked at it as going out and recruiting the best available athletes," Barry Switzer said once. "That's what we believed in, and it was the right thing to do."

Can't Block, Can't Win

Think before you speak. Always good words to heed when it comes to the sporting arena. Despite being a veteran Division-I coach, Pepper Rodgers found that out the hard way in 1968.

Rodgers let his mouth get away from him during an interview held the week prior to the annual Big Eight showdown between his third-ranked Kansas club and Oklahoma. And it would prove costly when the Sooners got wind of his remarks.

The undefeated Jayhawks had a pair of defensive ends in John Zook and Vernon Vanoy, both of whom would someday enjoy successful NFL careers. Rodgers was so confident that his talented bookends would ravage the Sooner offense that he told the Lawrence media as long as Mike Harper was OU's fullback, the Sooners couldn't beat Kansas.

"Coach [Barry] Switzer heard about what Rodgers had said, and he played it up all week," said OU tailback Steve Owens, the man Harper was responsible for blocking for almost every down.

"Switzer drilled that into us all week, and Mike certainly took exception to the comment."

Once the game kicked off, it was obvious the entire OU team had taken the comment as a slap in the face. The Sooners took it to Rodgers' Jayhawks, stuffing Zook and Vanoy throughout. KU's dynamic duo combined for three tackles the entire afternoon, as Owens ran 37 times for 157 yards, mostly behind Harper.

During the aftermath of OU's 27-23 victory, Harper shook hands with Rodgers and said, "I guess I proved you wrong today."

No doubt.

Hard to Know

Chuck Fairbanks wasn't one to mince words with coaches or his players. He was often described as suspicious, aloof, hard to get to know, never too friendly and downright mean. He was also a very good football coach, and he proved that during the six seasons he served as the top man at Oklahoma.

His record during that period was a sparkling 49-18-1. He was in charge when the Sooners transformed their offense into a juggernaut via the wishbone. His staff brought in the Selmon brothers—Lucious, Lee Roy and Dewey—and he helped turn the OU program into a budding national power. "Chuck was a tough son of a gun, just like the rest of his staff. He was a disciple of Jim Mackenzie, who was a disciple of Bear Bryant. And everyone saw what Bear was like in the *Junction Boys*," said quarterback Bobby Warmack. "Chuck wouldn't hardly say two words to you, but when he did say something you listened. He was hard, but fair—always fair."

Fairbanks surrounded himself with one of the best young staffs in college football, including Barry Switzer, Pat James, Galen Hall and Larry Lacewell. He always had the respect of his staff and players, according to quarterback Jack Mildren.

"Chuck could be a distant figure, but he never seemed that way to me personally," added Mildren. "He didn't talk a lot, but there was no doubt he was in charge."

Giving It His Best Shot

It's very rare that a big-time recruit in any sport slips through the cracks and winds up on the roster of a school that had no idea of the depth of his talents. Derland Moore was the exception to that rule.

In the summer of 1969, Norman hosted a Region 8 AAU track and field meet that included competitors from Oklahoma, Arkansas, Missouri and Kansas. Serving as one of the rules officials, OU track coach J. D. Martin made his way from event to event, overseeing the competition, at least until he got sidetracked.

Standing near the shot put area, Martin watched as a six-foot-five, 250-pound youngster named Derland Moore put on a show. Said Martin, "This big kid was chunking it out there pretty good, somewhere around 60 feet. He was very impressive."

Martin introduced himself to Moore, who had just graduated from high school in Poplar Bluff, Missouri, and asked him where he was going to college, thinking that he must have already signed with Missouri or Arkansas. To Martin's surprise, Moore said he had not yet found the right place.

"The kid said he wanted to throw, but that he really wanted to play football, too," said Martin. "I couldn't believe no one had signed him yet. I told him Oklahoma would be the perfect place for him to do both."

Minutes later, Martin was desperately trying to track down an OU football coach to help persuade Moore to sign with OU. He finally got freshman coach Don Jimerson on the phone and explained the situation.

"I asked Don to give him a quick tour and to tell him all about the football program. Just talk him into coming here and I'd give him a track scholarship," said Martin.

Before climbing back on a bus for Poplar Bluff, Moore told Martin if his dad said it was OK, he'd go to school there. A follow-up call a few days later confirmed the good news, and Moore showed up that fall ready to play football.

"Derland really wasn't recruited much out of high school. He played football, and he was a track guy who somehow didn't attract a lot of attention," said Barry Switzer, who was an OU assistant when Moore showed up in 1969. "All of the sudden he squatted down there and started beating people up. We found out real fast just how good he was."

Moore, who played defensive tackle, was big and strong with great quickness. The entire OU staff was stunned at how athletic this walk-on kid really was.

"Switzer called me after the team's first practice in pads and asked me where I found this kid because he was manhandling all of their All-Americans," said Martin. "Derland ended up being a good thrower in college, but football was his true calling. And soon after his freshman season he received a football scholarship."

Moore wound up being a three-year starter, earning All-Big Eight honors twice and All-America honors as a senior in 1972. He was a second-round NFL draft pick by New Orleans that year and went on to enjoy a 13-year career with the Saints.

"That's unheard of," added Switzer. "A walk-on who turned out to be a first- or second-round draft pick in the NFL. But Derland was the real deal."

Owens to the Rescue

When Barry Switzer and Larry Lacewell recount their days as assistant coaches at Oklahoma, both are quick to point to Steve Owens as one of the main reasons they roamed the sidelines in Norman for so many years.

The 1969 season is memorable basically because of Owens' Herculean efforts on a team that would eventually finish just 6-4 and fail to earn a bowl berth. It was a time when coach Chuck Fairbanks and his staff were under fire and many believed a new regime would be running the program to start the new decade.

In the season finale at Stillwater, the Sooners and Bedlam rival Cowboys hooked up in a toe-to-toe slugfest that saw Owens carry the ball a record 55 times for 261 yards. The senior back had 20 carries and 97 yards in the third quarter alone. And still the Sooners trailed 21-14.

"Steve did it all that day. He had all of those carries, and I think he even made a couple of special teams tackles," recalled Lacewell, the Sooners' defensive coordinator. "We always knew Steve was physically tougher than anyone else on the field, and that day he proved it over and over. It was amazing to watch."

Owens, who had won the Heisman Trophy a week earlier, was in the process of changing the course of OU football history. After helping the Sooners regain a 28-21 edge, an exhausted Owens watched anxiously as OSU scored in the final two minutes and lined up for what could be a game-winning two-point conversion.

"We really needed to win the game because there had been talk of firing our coaching staff that week," said Owens. "We, as players, really wanted to win, and every one of us did everything in our power to make that happen."

That everyone included backup defensive end Albert Qualls, whom Lacewell surprisingly substituted in for All-American Steve Zabel, just for the conversion attempt. Qualls chased OSU quarterback Bob Cutburth down from behind, forcing a fumble that OU's Johnny Watson recovered to ultimately preserve the victory.

The coaching staff was retained for the 1970 season and the nucleus of that group would later win three national championships with Switzer as head coach.

Who Called Timeout?

At one point of the 1969 Bedlam game, Oklahoma running back Steve Owens had carried the ball close to a dozen straight plays. The Sooners were driving, and momentum had shifted to their side.

But Owens was exhausted, and he could barely breathe when he stumbled back to the huddle after another bruising carry.

"I told our quarterback Jack Mildren we were going to have to call timeout because I needed a break. So he called timeout," recalled Owens, who finished with 55 carries for 261 yards that day.

Suddenly, offensive coordinator Barry Switzer is screaming at the coaches on the sidelines over their headsets, trying to find out who jeopardized their momentum by calling timeout.

"Jack got on the headset and explained it was me who wanted the rest, and Switzer screamed back down, 'Tell Owens this is the last game of the season, he'll have the rest of the year to rest,'" laughed Owens.

The Sooners eventually scored on the drive and won the game 28-27.

Steve Owens vs. Nebraska. *Photo courtesy of the University of Oklahoma*

CHAPTER FIVE

The 1970s

Popsicles and Gatorade

AT SOME POINT during every Oklahoma practice the freshman receivers would break from their normal routine and take part in one-on-one drills against the varsity secondary. It was a chance for the young guys to measure up against some of the best defensive backs in the country.

Chuck Fairbanks' Sooners had already opened the 1972 season with a 49-0 shellacking of Utah State, so the starting lineups were pretty much solidified as they ran through preparations for their week two opponent, Oregon.

Tinker Owens joined the OU program as a running back, but had decided to test his talents as a receiver since the Sooners were already loaded in the backfield. The pressures of following in big brother Steve Owens' footsteps were a bit daunting, especially as a freshman.

Little did young Tinker know that his life was about to change as he made his way down to the field for one-on-one drills one afternoon that week. Owens demonstrated soft hands and deceptive speed as he scored three touchdowns against starting cornerback Kenny Pope, with Fairbanks looking on.

Afterward, as the freshmen were being dismissed, Fairbanks told Owens to go get a popsicle and Gatorade.

"That's what the varsity players had at the break," said Owens. "I'm not very smart, so I walked over to get a popsicle and drink and started walking to the locker room."

Fairbanks yelled out to Owens, telling him to stay out with the veterans. Then after practice Owens was asked to report to assistant coach Galen Hall about playing with the varsity against Oregon.

"Coach Fairbanks had seen me that day in one-on-one drills and wanted to see what I could do with the varsity. I was just in the right place at the right time. It was almost by accident," offered Owens.

Thrilled with his new role, Owens never dreamed he would play against Oregon that week. He watched intently as the Sooners slowly began dismantling the Ducks, and suddenly the unexpected occurred. Receiver John Carroll came up lame and Fairbanks began yelling for Owens to go into the game.

"I was in shock and I had laid my helmet down somewhere and couldn't find it. So I'm running around searching through all of the helmets," recalled Owens. "It was crazy."

Once Owens finally got to the huddle, another surprise was waiting—quarterback Dave Robertson called a pass play. Trying to remember his routes, Owens lined up and ran an out pattern. As he turned he saw the ball diving toward the ground, so he stretched out and made a beautiful catch just inches off the turf. The 10-yard completion was good for a first down.

As members of the press began checking their lineup cards for the name of this new acrobatic pass catcher, they discovered there was no number 11 listed. Even the public address announcer had no idea who the mystery man was. Later, someone radioed down to the sideline to get number 11's name.

Tinker Owens. An amazing start to an All-America career.

No More Little Red

During the Vietnam War, the National Indian Youth Council organized protests of Oklahoma's official mascot, Little Red, saying the university's depiction of an Indian in costume was stereotypical and demeaning. A debate ensued with OU president J. Herbert Holloman stuck in the middle.

Little Red, originated in the 1950s by OU's public relations office to complement the football program's famous "Big Red" nickname, was officially sanctioned as the school's mascot in 1957 with Anadarko, Oklahoma, native Phil Waller in costume.

"The administration was 100 percent behind me. The response was absolutely marvelous," Waller said. "I was treated with the utmost respect."

Little Red became a popular feature at OU home games, dressed in a war bonnet, fancy dance-bustle, moccasins, furs and traditional beadwork. He helped rev up crowds with his well-versed routine for almost 15 years before the protests began.

"I'm not sure I followed some of the logic about how (Little Red) was demeaning to Indians," said Kirke Kickingbird, a Kiowa tribal member who served as the famed mascot from 1963-68. "When you look at mascots, it's usually something people admire. I think that was the whole purpose of putting Little Red into place."

Even though Hollomon officially banished Little Red on April 17, 1970, the longtime tradition would not die so easily. Randy Palmer, a Kiowa tribal member and student from Anadarko, danced as Little Red for three more seasons before demand finally faded and the mascot was retired.

The Greatest Game Ever Played

Oklahoma's wishbone offense was humming as the second-ranked Sooners cruised through the 1971 season headed for a showdown with No. 1 Nebraska. The game would not only determine the Big Eight title, but possibly the national championship.

The lineups read like a *Who's Who*, with Greg Pruitt, Johnny Rodgers, Rich Glover and Jack Mildren topping the marquee.

In what became known as the "Game of the Century," Nebraska defeated the second-ranked Sooners in a 35-31 victory on Thanksgiving Day. It was one of the most memorable collegiate football games in history, said Penn State coach Joe Paterno, whose words echoed the sentiments of the entire football world.

For OU defensive coordinator Larry Lacewell, it was a bitter disappointment. While the Sooner defense held the Cornhuskers to one offensive touchdown and led 17-14 at the half, Lacewell admittedly called a conservative game defensively after the intermission, and it cost Oklahoma dearly.

The Sooner offense, led by quarterback Mildren, was rolling up yards and points, but they were getting little help in the way of defensive stops.

"That game taught me a lot of lessons as a defensive coordinator," said Lacewell. "It taught me to be maybe a little more reckless in big situations, like third and long or third and five. I should have had our guys go after them a little more."

But as it turned out, the undefeated Huskers managed to convert basically every critical third-down situation they faced. It slowly drained the life from OU's attack unit and set them up for the kill with a 12-play, 74-yard fourth-quarter scoring drive.

"It was a case of which team had the ball last," OU coach Chuck Fairbanks would say. "If we would have had enough time, I'm certain we would have scored."

Unfortunately, OU got the ball back deep in its own territory with just 1:38 remaining. The wishbone offense wasn't built for the two-minute drill, and it showed as the Sooners turned it over on downs after just four plays.

"It was a quintessential college football game," added Mildren. "I certainly can understand how it was voted the 'greatest game ever played.'"

On Again, Off Again

When it came to practice, linemen Terry Webb and Jaime Melendez were less than enthusiastic. Practically every day at some point during workouts, either one or the other would do something to cause offensive line coach Gene Hochevar to reconsider their starting status.

"I must have kicked both of those guys out of the lineup or off the team a dozen times each," admitted Hochevar. "But every time they'd go to Barry [Switzer] and talk him into letting them back on the team, which I knew he would. The funny thing was, as uninspired as they were during practice, they were both fantastic when Saturday rolled around.

"They just hated to practice."

Halftime Break

The halftime locker room can be a rather intense place depending on how a team played during the first 30 minutes of action. Many spirited speeches have been delivered during the intermission with hopes that fortunes would be altered or sustained.

That was not the case when Oklahoma met Oregon in the 1975 season opener. The Sooners had rolled out to a 44-0 lead by the time the two teams exited Owen Field for the break.

As was tradition, OU's players went to the locker room and its coaches went to the coaches' offices to talk strategy before joining the players. This time, however, several minutes went by and no one made a move toward the locker room. Barry Switzer and his staff kicked back and ordered up some lunch.

After a few more minutes, assistant coach Bobby Proctor stood up and asked if they were going to the locker room to coach the players. Everybody just turned around and looked at him.

Finally, Switzer said, "Bobby, if you want to, you can go coach them. But if you don't mind, we're going to stay here and eat these hot dogs and drink these cokes."

Avoiding Disaster

The final stages of recruiting were winding down, and OU assistant Larry Lacewell had just a few loose ends to shore up before turning his focus to other things. Little did he know that history was about to be made, and it didn't necessarily include his Sooners.

Lacewell rolled in to Eufaula, Oklahoma, in mid-afternoon, fully expecting to sign a player named Lucious Selmon. Although he had pursued the defensive prospect without much fanfare, Lacewell figured the kid was in the bag.

"When I pulled up, I saw Lucious with Colorado coach Eddie Crowder. His school books were in Crowder's car, and I immediately knew we might be in trouble," explained Lacewell. "I didn't even bother having Chuck [Fairbanks] come with me, because I didn't think Lucious was interested in going anywhere else. I was embarrassed because I really thought I was going to lose this guy."

Lacewell was meeting with the Selmons later that evening, so he decided to grab something to eat with Crowder at a local restaurant. During their meal, Crowder excused himself to make a phone call, and Lacewell knew was what coming next.

"The phone was in the back of the restaurant, and I walked back around the corner and listened to everything Crowder told the Selmons I was going to say and ask," said Lacewell. "So I had all kinds of ammo when I went to their house that night. The main thing I told Lucious was the best reason to pick Oklahoma is because it's the better school. And that was true.

"Then I told his mother that it was 109 miles from Eufaula to Norman and it was a lot farther than that to Boulder. I asked her how in the world she was ever going to watch her son play, especially toting two other boys along. That was a key issue."

In the end, Selmon signed with Oklahoma, and two years later, Lee Roy and Dewey followed their older brother to Norman. During the five years that followed, the Sooners went 41-6-1 and won two national titles.

"At the time, we didn't realize what we were getting. If I hadn't listened to Eddie Crowder that day, history may have been changed," added Lacewell. "The good Lord looked down on us that day. And then for us to get all three Selmons—that seemed hardly fair."

The Wishbone

The 1969 season, even with the Heisman Trophy performance of running back Steve Owens, was viewed as a major disappointment in and around OU circles. Two years removed from capping a 10-1 season with a victory over No. 2 Tennessee in the Orange Bowl, the Sooners had become one-dimensional and a bit predicable in their veer offense.

While archrival Texas was winning a national championship in '69, coach Chuck Fairbanks' staff was worried about keeping their jobs. A 28-27 victory over Oklahoma State in the season finale had provided a short reprieve, but the natives were growing restless.

After watching the Longhorns run the wishbone to absolute perfection during their title run, OU offensive coordinator Barry Switzer started wondering why the Sooners shouldn't borrow a little from their southern neighbors.

"Hell, Texas was scoring half-a-hundred on every team they played. They were running all over the yard and no one could stop them," recalled Switzer. "I looked at their roster and I looked at ours, and it was pretty clear we had better athletes than Texas did. So why not switch to the wishbone?"

Switzer suggested the change in a meeting with Fairbanks, and it was discussed again during a team meeting after the Sooners had started 2-1 in 1970.

"I basically talked Chuck into it," added Switzer. "I told him if we wanted to save our jobs he'd better make the switch to the wishbone."

On October 10, 1970, Oklahoma debuted its version of the wishbone in a 41-9 loss to—who else—Texas.

"To change in the middle of the season, that's a terrifically tough decision. I found it hard to fathom why," admitted quarterback Jack Mildren. "It was a tumultuous two weeks, to say the least. To install a new offense and then go play a team like Texas wasn't easy.

"But the coaching staff's jobs were on the line. They felt they needed to do something drastic, and I think they deserve a lot of credit for having the courage and vision to make the change."

Despite the Sooners' lack of immediate success, they stuck with the triple-option attack over the next 16 seasons, winning three national titles during that span.

Policing the Athletic Dorms

One semester there was a problem with thefts occurring in the athletic dorms. Several items had come up missing from various players' rooms, and it was cause for concern among the Selmon brothers, who were the self-appointed authority for the Wilkinson Center.

Lucious, Dewey and Lee Roy were determined to find out who was stealing from their teammates, and they set out on an in-house crime investigation.

A few days later during roll call for one of coach Barry Switzer's team meetings, a certain halfback from Houston was curiously missing. Switzer called out the kid's name several times and then began to inquire about his whereabouts.

"One player stood up and said, 'He's on a bus back to Houston, Coach,'" explained Switzer. "I asked why and the kid said Lucious, Lee Roy and Dewey took him down to the bus station and felt like it was the best thing for him to go back home."

Earlier that day, the brothers' investigation had led them to the player in question's room, where they discovered all of the stolen items in his closet.

"They had some clues who it was, and they took the door off the hinges to find out," added Switzer. "When they saw it was him, they packed his bags and drove him to the bus station. That was all that needed to be said."

Funny Man

The 1975 season was full of surprises, mostly magical and occasionally sobering. Oklahoma was on its way to a second straight national championship, and thanks to George Davis, there was a bit of comic relief to help counter the pressure when it got too intense.

Davis, a backup linebacker and the younger brother of former quarterback Steve Davis, spent much of his spare time entertaining his teammates with a unique sense of humor and timing.

"George was the team funny man. He was a real character and he was good for team morale," said teammate Tinker Owens. "He was always good for a laugh."

Davis got into the habit of making sensational entrances at the regular Friday walkthrough practice. The players loved it. One week, he showed up in an ambulance. The next week, he was piloted in on a helicopter that landed on Owen Field. Then there was the horse.

The list goes on and on.

"Everybody knew George had something big planned, and we all looked forward to it," added Owens. "He had quite an imagination."

Beating Texas

Oklahoma made a habit of finding ways to beat rival Texas during the Barry Switzer era. A perfect example of that unfolded during the 1974 Red River Showdown in Dallas.

Installed as 21-point favorites prior to the game, the Sooners played more like an underdog for the opening three quarters. Three turnovers in Texas territory, coupled with several other blunders, left Switzer's crew in a 13-7 hole.

"We just couldn't seem to do anything right during the first three quarters," said quarterback Steve Davis.

Suddenly, the realization that an undefeated season and a shot at the national title was slipping away kicked in. A dose of "Sooner Magic" did the rest.

Billy Brooks got the comeback started when he took a reverse handoff from Davis 40 yards for a touchdown to open the fourth quarter. The game remained tied when OU failed to convert the extra point, but momentum had swung.

OU's Lee Roy Selmon recovered an Earl Campbell fumble on the following series, setting up a 37-yard field goal by Tony DiRienzo with 5:25 remaining. Selmon would help close the door by recovering another Campbell fumble in the closing moments.

I'm Coming Home

During the days and hours after being told his team was changing from its veer offense to a run-oriented attack called the wishbone, Greg Pruitt sat down and contemplated his future at Oklahoma. He came to the conclusion that he didn't like what he envisioned.

"I just looked at it as an offense a wide receiver would get lost in. Everything was run, run, run, and I didn't see a whole lot of future for a guy who caught passes," explained Pruitt. "I was very resistant to change. I was disappointed about not starting."

So the fledgling sophomore called home and told his mother he was going to leave OU and find another school. Maggie Pruitt didn't want to hear it. In not so many words, she told her talented son that she didn't raise any quitters and that he'd better rethink what she felt was a rash decision.

"Greg didn't realize it, because all he saw at the time was the fact he was being moved out of the starting lineup as a receiver. But it was a move that he would ultimately take full advantage of," explained OU coach Barry Switzer.

Switzer, of course, was right. Pruitt made a better-than-expected transition to halfback, and by his junior season had become one of the most feared running backs in the country. He ran for 1,665 yards that season (1971) and averaged an NCAA-record 9.41 yards per carry.

"As it turned out, staying at OU was the best thing that could have happened to me," added Pruitt, who finished his collegiate career with 2,844 rushing yards and 38 touchdowns.

Waiting His Turn

Oklahoma's roster was so deep and so strong during the 1970s that many players who might have been stars at some other school were relegated to the bench. Jimmy Rogers was one of those "what if" guys.

Stuck behind players like Joe Washington, Billy Sims and David Overstreet for his entire Sooner career, Rogers got very few chances to strut his stuff as a running back. Ironically, Rogers was still selected by New Orleans in the 1980 NFL draft, and he played four seasons with the Saints.

Not Exactly Part of the Team?

During the late 1960s and early '70s, when Oklahoma football was rediscovering the glory years of the Bud Wilkinson era, a problem evolved, albeit a small one. Kids began walking on for the football team who had only one thing in mind—to be a part of the team photo. A day or two after the photo session, they would turn in their gear and disappear.

Back then, the Sooners held their picture day a few days before preseason camp started. So walk-ons and other non-scholarship players were included in the picture day process.

"It got to be a problem, because these kids would act like they were walking on just to be in the photo and then quit the team before practice began," said former OU sports information director Mike Treps. "All they were interested in was showing their buddies they played football for OU, and they'd have the photo as proof."

Not that OU was lax about letting just anyone sign up to play football, but it had to start doing more in-depth background checks on potential walk-ons.

Rolling Over

Barry Switzer's staff was forever making recruiting trips deep into Texas, searching for the Billy Simses and Brian Bosworths of the world. A frequent stop was Houston, where OU booster Sam Mason would fly the staff to various destinations in his private jet.

On one occasion, Switzer, Jerry Pettibone, Gene Hochevar and Wendell Mosely were flying with Mason, who was a pilot, when they decided to have a little fun with Mosely. Switzer went into the cockpit and asked Mason to do a rollover maneuver to see how Mosely would react.

Back in the cabin, Mosely and his fellow assistants were sipping cocktails and smoking cigars, discussing the flight home. Mosely had just taken a big puff off his cigar when the plane made a big roll to the right.

"Wendell swallowed that smoke, completely turned white and about bit the end of his cigar off," recalled Hochevar, laughing as he relived the moment.

About 30 minutes later, Mason pulled the cockpit curtain back and informed the staff that a thunderstorm was on the horizon and the plane would have to jockey around it.

"Sam tells us if we go around the storm we might be cutting it a little close on fuel, but he's not too worried about it. He said he could put us down in Dallas and refuel, but it would make us late getting back to Norman," explained Hochevar.

About then, Mosely perked up in his seat, noticed no one else was going to debate the options and said: "Put this son of a bitch down. The only time you've got too much gas is when you're on fire."

Of course, Switzer and company, having put Mason up to the joke, were rolling in the aisles by the time Mosely had finished expressing his concerns.

Keeping it Snappy

When a series of mysterious ailments sidelined quarterback Dean Blevins in the early part of the 1976 season, coach Barry Switzer turned to sophomore signal caller Thomas Lott. With just two days of preparation, Lott found himself under the microscope as the Sooners traveled to Dallas for their annual showdown with Texas.

Keeping things as simple as possible until Lott fully learned the offense, the Sooners used the word "hut" for their snap signal. And most of the time, it was simply on one "hut."

"As we did that, the defensive teams we were playing began to adjust to it," explained former offensive lineman Mike Vaughn. "Trying to get an advantage, a lot of the linebackers on the other side were calling out signals. It was drawing us offsides quite a bit. As soon as Thomas started his cadence, you'd hear 'hut, hut.'"

Obviously, the Sooners were forced to vary their snap count after the penalties got out of hand.

Sooner Magic

Oklahoma football fans had grown accustomed to winning programs over the 25 seasons that preceded the Barry Switzer era. Other than a few lean years in the 1960s, the Sooners had racked up victories at a record pace, winning three national championships and countless conference titles along the way.

That was Bud Wilkinson's legacy.

But Switzer's teams would add a new dimension to Sooner lore, and it would be known as "Sooner Magic."

Switzer defined Sooner Magic as "good players making big plays in critical situations." His OU teams made a habit out of producing clutch performances and sensational comebacks.

The term "Sooner Magic" actually originated from the OU-Nebraska series and the fact that the Sooners routinely found ways to frustrate their rivals from the north, usually with some kind of late-game heroics.

"You just knew their fans were sitting in the stands saying, 'Oh no, they're doing it to us again,'" said Switzer, who owned a 12-5 record against Nebraska.

Good Company

It's very rare that three players from the same university are selected in the first round of the National Football League's annual draft. But that was the case on April 8, 1976, when Lee Roy Selmon, Joe Washington and Billy Brooks were the first, fourth and 11th overall picks by Tampa Bay, San Diego and Cincinnati, respectively.

Selmon, a two-time consensus All-America defensive end, was the first Sooner since Heisman Trophy winner Billy Vessels to be selected as the overall number-one pick.

Centers Stick Together

President Gerald Ford helped get the annual Red River Rivalry under way in 1976, participating as the guest of honor in the pregame coin toss. Afterward, he joined some fellow dignitaries in the Cotton Bowl stands and watched as 16th-ranked Texas, on the strength of two Russell Erxleben field goals, had the No. 3 Sooners on the ropes deep into the fourth quarter.

But just when it looked like the Longhorns would pull off the upset, OU recovered a fumble that set up the game-tying scoring drive. Suddenly, the spotlight shifted to the foot of Uwe von Schamann, who missed only one point-after kick during his entire collegiate career. Unfortunately for the Sooners, von Schamann never got the chance to give OU the lead.

"Basically, all we had to do was kick the extra point to win the game. But it didn't happen," said von Schamann.

Center Kevin Craig's snap was high and hard, and holder Bud Hebert could not handle it. Hebert tracked down the loose ball and tried to pass into the end zone, but it fell incomplete, leaving the two rivals deadlocked at 6-6.

Craig had been a team manager until Barry Switzer noticed him zipping some deep snaps one day before practice. The following week, Switzer installed Craig as his new special teams center.

A few days after the game, Craig received a personal letter from President Ford containing words of encouragement, including the closing line, "Centers have to stick together." Ford had played center for Michigan's undefeated national football championship teams in 1932-33.

Climb Aboard

Before the University of Nebraska made serious weight training a routine part of college football programs, most Big Eight schools like Oklahoma featured very substandard equipment in that area. Even into the mid-1970s the Sooners were lagging behind in the strength conditioning department.

Underneath Memorial Stadium, in an old 30x30 storage room, is where the Sooners worked on their lifting. There were two large universal machines located there, only one of which was maintained in working order at all times, and two sets of free weights.

"The Selmon brothers would come in there and do reps with all of the weight on every part of the machine," said All-America receiver Tinker Owens. "There wasn't enough weight for those guys."

Lee Roy Selmon improvised when working on strengthening his lower extremities. One day, Selmon had maxed out the leg-lift portion of the machine, so he had OU kicker Tony DiRienzo sit on the bar to provide even more resistance.

It's a little-known fact that DiRienzo played such a major role in Selmon's success.

The Minister of Offense

There was nothing flashy about Steve Davis. He wasn't particularly fast and didn't have a great arm. The Sallisaw, Oklahoma, product looked more like, well, a choirboy than a college quarterback.

Fact was, Davis was a Baptist minister who was as quiet-natured and unassuming off the field as he was ferocious and unflappable as a player.

So what made Davis so good?

"He could move the football team, bottom line," said OU coach Barry Switzer. "Steve wasn't the best athlete, but he turned to gold when he hit that field. He was smart, confident and he didn't make mistakes. That's the definition of a good quarterback."

Little did anyone know, when Davis earned the starting job in 1973, that he would lead the Sooners to a pair of national titles and an overall record of 32-1-1.

No Room in the Backfield

When George Cumby arrived in Norman prior to the 1975 season, he had high hopes of becoming part of the next generation of great running backs at Oklahoma. A native of Moore Station City, Texas, he was six feet, 200 pounds, with a sprinter's speed.

Unfortunately for Cumby, his timing, in terms of breaking into the OU backfield, was less than perfect. Fellow freshman Kenny King and several veterans were the front-runners for the starting job, and it became apparent that Cumby, despite all of his physical assets, was destined for the bench.

To make matters worse, Cumby broke his collarbone early in his freshman season and then broke it again the following spring.

"It was a situation where George was stuck behind a couple of guys who were better than he was as a fullback. Plus, he got hurt and that put him behind," said OU coach Barry Switzer. "But he was such a good athlete, we figured we could find a place for him on the field, even if it meant moving him to defense."

Switzer asked Cumby to try defense for a couple of weeks, and he eventually made the move to linebacker in the spring of 1976.

"Initially, I didn't want to move. I told him I felt I was a running back and that's where I wanted to play," said Cumby. "But he told me to think about it, and I decided to give it try."

Oh, what a try. Cumby, under the tutelage of assistant coach Warren Harper, made the transition look easy. And when Daryl Hunt injured his knee, he suddenly was at the top of the depth chart.

"I never looked back. I really just wanted to play, and moving to linebacker gave me that chance," added Cumby. "I think it worked out pretty well."

A rare combination of speed and strength, Cumby was Big Eight Defensive Newcomer of the Year as a sophomore, and he twice earned the conference's top defensive player award during his career. By the time he left for the NFL after the '79 season, Cumby was a two-time All-American and fourth on OU's career tackles list with 405.

No Bowl Game, No Problem

After the NCAA slapped sanctions on Oklahoma for transcript violations during Chuck Fairbanks' final season as head coach and six All-Big Eight players departed, it was widely believed that the Sooners were in for hard times while they waded through three seasons of probation.

But Barry Switzer believed differently. After taking over for Fairbanks prior to the 1973 season, the 35-year-old skipper was confident in his program's talent and resolve.

"I knew we weren't going to roll over and play dead just because someone said so," recalled Switzer, whose '73 squad finished 10-0-1, its only blemish a 7-7 tie against No. 1 Southern Cal.

The following season, Switzer's Sooners forged a perfect 11-0 regular-season record and then sat back and watched how the bowl games unfolded.

College football writer Hershel Nissenson publicly stated that the Associated Press was not a "policing agency" and therefore it would not punish college football teams by excluding them from its weekly polls. The Sooners had been in the top 10 all season and when the final AP poll was released after the 1974 bowl season, Oklahoma was voted No. 1, despite being on NCAA probation.

Block That Kick!

Any person who claimed to be an Oklahoma football fan in 1977 will always remember what he or she was doing on September 24 of that year. More specifically where they were at the moment that Uwe von Schamann kicked a game-winning 41-yard field goal to beat fourth-ranked Ohio State, 29-28.

It was the equivalent of the 1971 "Game of the Century" between OU and Nebraska, only this time the Sooners had plenty to celebrate as the final gun sounded.

OU built a 20-0 lead that day, but injuries to quarterback Thomas Lott and running back Billy Sims helped alter the two teams' fortunes, at least for a while. Woody Hayes' Buckeyes stormed back, scoring 28 unanswered points, and it looked as if the third-ranked Sooners would leave Columbus disappointed.

But "Sooner Magic" was lurking in the shadows.

Plenty of things had to happen to set up von Schamann's heroics, beginning with Phil Tabor forcing a Greg Castignola fumble that teammate Reggie Kinlaw recovered to give OU new life late in the game. Moments later with 1:29 remaining, Elvis Peacock scored on an option pitch right to cut the lead to 28-26. But the Sooners' comeback stalled when they failed to convert the potential game-tying two-point attempt.

On von Schamann's ensuing on-side kick, the ball glanced off of an Ohio State player and Mike Babb recovered for OU near midfield. Backup quarterback Dean Blevins connected with Steve Rhodes for an 18-yard gain, and the Sooners ran the ball three straight times (two by Kenny King), advancing to the OSU 24 with six seconds left.

"We called time out to stop the clock and set up the kick and when we got ready to go, Ohio State called a timeout," said von Schamann, recalling Hayes' freeze tactics. "During the second timeout it was so loud, it was the first time I ever remembered noticing the crowd."

In that instant, as 90,000 Buckeye faithful joined to chant "Block that kick, block that kick," von Schamann felt his confidence level rising. In fact, he was so aware of the moment that he turned to the loudest portion of the stadium and helped lead the deafening chant.

"I had dreamed about being in a situation like that, so I had prepared myself mentally," offered von Schamann. "I felt all along like I was going to make it."

And that he did, splitting the uprights from 41 yards away. Good.

"You've never heard a stadium that big get so quiet so fast," said OU coach Barry Switzer. "It was a great finish to one of the greatest games I was ever involved in."

A Lott to Remember

Oklahoma was on the verge of signing San Antonio high school star Thomas Lott during the 1975 recruiting season. Lott scheduled a press conference to announce his decision, and OU coaches Barry Switzer and Wendell Mosely flew to Texas to seal the deal.

Just before the big moment, Switzer turned to Mosely and asked for the letter of intent. Mosely replied, "I didn't bring them. I thought you had them." Mosely had basically forgotten the most important item for the trip, and they had to fly back to Oklahoma to get the proper paperwork.

The next day, Switzer made it back down to San Antonio and signed Lott to play for his Sooners.

The Hair and the Toupee

Charlie North, who coached tight ends at OU from 1979-94, put his sense of humor on display occasionally, including one time after he and a few members of Barry Switzer's staff had participated in a high school coaching clinic at nearby Purcell, Oklahoma. The group stopped in at a local watering hole afterward, and North went to work, asking the barmaid if she had seen his brother hanging around. The unsuspecting girl said she had not seen him.

A bit later, North exited the bar, went to his car and tossed his toupee in the trunk. After waiting a while, he made his return, now sporting a new look, and promptly asked the same barmaid if she had seen his brother. Without hesitation, she went into the whole story about how "his brother" was just here a few minutes earlier and she would keep an eye out for him if he returned.

Of course, North's fellow assistants each struggled to keep a straight face while listening to the girl fall for the trickery.

Different Kind of Rug

When Oklahoma went to artificial turf in 1969, Memorial Stadium took on a new and seemingly improved look. It was ideal for running, and that's exactly what the Sooners needed with their wishbone offense.

But while OU's speedsters got speedier, there were trade-offs that didn't necessarily sit well with the players, such as the injury factor. As the original turf got older, it became so coarse that players were more worried about incurring serious rug burns and gaping strawberries than being pounded by an angry 260-pound opponent.

"They used to paint the center of the field and end zones, and every year, it got harder and harder and more abrasive," said OU assistant Bobby Proctor. "For a while it seemed we had more guys in the training room for scrapes and burns than anything else. It was bad."

OU finally replaced the old turf with "Super Turf" prior to the 1981 season. It looked better and had better padding, but it still managed to take a layer or two of skin if a player hit it just right.

Too Slow

Daryl Hunt was no speedster when he was recruited by Oklahoma in 1975. And after suffering a severe knee injury during the spring prior to his sophomore year, his wheels got even slower. He was timed at five seconds flat regularly during the team's 40-yard sprint drills.

When Hunt ended his Sooner career after the 1978 season, he did so as the school's all-time leading tackler. Not to mention that he was a two-time All-American and a player Barry Switzer described as "one of the toughest hard-nosed tacklers in the game."

But what about that five-flat thing?

"It's true, Daryl ran a 5.0 40," said teammate and fellow linebacker George Cumby. "He absolutely had no speed. But he was six-five and 225 pounds and his football instincts were incredible. Here I was with 4.4, 4.5 speed and Daryl and I would end up at the ball carrier at the same time, play after play.

"He was amazing. He was a great student of the game and he really was able to make that work to his advantage."

Wanted: Punter

One game into the 1975 season, Barry Switzer's Oklahoma squad was still trying to work out details with its special teams units. Tony DiRienzo was a solid place kicker, but senior Jim Littrell, the Sooners' regular punter, developed a bad case of the shanks and couldn't seem to shake them.

Switzer was desperate, so he announced after practice one day that he wanted anyone and everyone who had ever punted the ball before to hang around and try out for punter.

Among those who tested their legs that day were Joe Washington, Kirk Killion, Craig Lund and Tinker Owens.

"We started kicking the ball around, and I'm just booming it," Owens said. "I was kicking it better than I had ever punted in high school. So I ended up getting the job.

"I remember looking over at Joe [Washington] and he's all smiles, so I asked him what was up. He said he was happy I got the job because no one else out there really wanted it."

Owens, who would average just over 36 yards a punt that season, later admitted his job was to catch the ball and get rid of it.

"Our defense was so good we figured as long as I gave them a chance to stop our opponents, we were in pretty good shape," smiled Owens.

No Pay, No Play?

Opening Saturday, 1973. The Barry Switzer era is about to begin at Oklahoma, as the Sooners load onto the team buses at their hotel in Temple, Texas, en route to Waco and a game with Baylor that afternoon. But Switzer was about to find out that even destined-to-be-legendary coaches aren't immune to the rising cost of collegiate athletics.

As the buses rolled into the stadium complex on the Baylor campus, they came to a gate area manned by a pair of fellows in charge of collecting parking fees. Instead of the gate opening up at the sight of the buses, the men approached the vehicles and requested payment from the stunned drivers.

After a few minutes of delay, OU athletic business manager Ken Farris got out to see what the problem was. A heated debate ensued with Farris explaining that visiting teams should never be asked to pay to park at the host's stadium. But the Baylor gate-keepers would not relent, and a flabbergasted Farris eventually coughed up the going rate.

By the end of the day, Oklahoma had gotten its money's worth via a 41-14 pounding of the Bears.

One Tough Mother

Defensive back Jerry Anderson was considered by many to be the toughest, meanest player to ever wear an Oklahoma uniform. He lit up opposing receivers with forearms and vicious hits, and he did it playing on basically one knee.

During his senior season in 1976, an examination determined that Anderson's anterior cruciate ligament in his right knee had deteriorated beyond repair. Despite playing in much pain, Anderson completed the season without missing a beat, according to assistant coach Bobby Proctor.

"He was unbelievably tough. That's what made him so good," said Proctor.

Hulk and Bulk

Look up the term "blue collar," and almost certainly the accompanying picture would be of Gerry Arnold and John Roush. The hard-working tandem played side by side at left guard and tackle, respectively, for parts of their three seasons at OU.

"If you gave those two an assignment, no matter what it was, they'd get it done 99 percent of the time," said OU offensive line coach Gene Hochevar, who dubbed the duo "Hulk" and "Bulk" during the 1973 season.

But according to Hochevar, the pair often provided comic relief, especially during games when they'd argue over offensive line calls and blocking assignments.

"It was a wonder they were on the same page as much as they were, because they were always going back and forth about something. They would break the huddle arguing and they would come back to the huddle arguing," laughed Hochevar. "But when it came to grinding it out in the trenches, they'd roll you up like a window shade. They got the job done."

Typical Wedge Breakers?

When people think of wedge breakers in football, images of wild-eyed kamikazes come to mind, aggressive players who propel themselves like missiles into harm's way on kickoffs. Quarterbacks usually don't fall into that category.

Scott Hill and Joe McReynolds did.

Both had come to Oklahoma as budding quarterbacks out of high school, bent on taking the reins of the Sooners' powerful wishbone offense. But it was on special teams where Hill and McReynolds first earned their stripes.

They both played with reckless abandon and became OU's ultimate wedge breakers during the 1975 season.

Polish, Not Practice

Billy Sims, David Overstreet, J. C. Watts, Thomas Lott, Kenny King, the list goes on and on. The amount of talent Oklahoma had on the offensive side of the football during the late 1970s was astounding.

Even more amazing was the fact Barry Switzer's wishbone juggernaut barely broke a sweat in practice, at least according to some members of Larry Lacewell's defensive unit.

"They'd call it polishing. Heck, they'd be eating dinner while the defense was still out practicing," laughed Sherwood Taylor, a three-year starting safety from Ada, Oklahoma. "That's how good those guys were. Didn't matter who they'd run out there, the talent level was unbelievable."

While the OU defense wasn't exactly considered a weak link during that period, it was more than happy to grind it out until dusk without facing the offense.

"We always said our team scrimmages were the toughest thing we did," added Taylor. "After going against that kind of talent, every other team we faced seemed easy by comparison."

The Omen

Saturday November 8, 1975—A day that will live in infamy as far as Oklahoma football lore is concerned.

Joe Washington. *Photo courtesy of the University of Oklahoma*

Barry Switzer's No. 1-ranked Sooners had beaten 28 consecutive opponents and were riding an unbeaten streak of 37 straight games. The defending national champs were prohibitive favorites and expected little resistance from an unheralded Kansas squad visiting Memorial Stadium that afternoon.

And as it turned out, the Sooners were halfway right. It wasn't the Jayhawks as much as themselves that they should've been concerned about. In a shocking performance, OU did little right on its way to a 23-3 upset loss.

What went wrong? The Sooners had a critical touchdown called back. They had a punt blocked that set up a KU touchdown. They fumbled it away four times, including once on the KU goal line. They also threw four interceptions and had a field goal blocked.

As a side note, early in the second quarter, sure-handed Tinker Owens dropped a Steve Davis pass. It was the only pass Owens dropped during his entire OU career.

Joe Washington knew at that moment the Sooners were in trouble.

"I knew we were going to lose that game after Tinker dropped the pass, because he never dropped passes, not even in practice," said Washington.

Despite the stunning loss, OU rebounded to win its final three games, including 14-6 over Michigan in the Orange Bowl, and earn the program's fifth national championship.

Moving on up (in a hurry)

On the opening day of spring practice in 1973, Mike Vaughn found himself checking out the depth chart for Oklahoma's offensive line. After giving the posted list of good once-over, the redshirt freshman spotted his name—seventh-team offensive tackle.

"Not exactly All-America material," joked Vaughn, reminiscing.

The 6-foot-6, 275-pound Ada product, who was coming off of winter shoulder surgery, spent the first three days of practice holding blocking dummies during drills for the offensive linemen.

"I knew the lower guys on the totem pole held the dummies, but I certainly didn't like it," he said. "I was getting pretty good at it after three days, but wave after wave of blockers hitting those dummies will wear on you pretty fast."

On the fourth day, the Sooners held a two-on-two drill, better known as the "Oklahoma Drill," where the linemen are filmed and graded while going head to head. Finally, Vaughn had a chance to showcase his skills, and he made the most of it.

By the time he showed up for practice the following day, he had leapfrogged to third on the depth chart.

That was the beginning of a very successful stay at Oklahoma. By the time Vaughn exited, he had earned All-Big Eight honors twice and All-America honors once. Not bad for a former seventh-teamer.

The "Beat Colorado Party"

The 1970 season figured to be pivotal in Oklahoma's football fortunes, as Chuck Fairbanks and his staff were coming off of a 6-4 campaign that saw them fail to earn a postseason bowl bid.

Three games into the fall, the Sooners decided to change offenses—opting for a the same wishbone attack archrival Texas had been deploying with great success the last few seasons. OU debuted its wishbone in a 41-9 loss to the Longhorns on October 10.

"We knew we were doing the right thing going to the wishbone, because we had the talent to run that offense. It was just a matter of time," said assistant coach Barry Switzer.

The problem was patience. OU fans didn't have any, and their "Chuck Chuck" campaign didn't exactly infect the young coaching staff with a lot of confidence.

"I was sitting in the office with Larry Lacewell and Jimmy Johnson, and I told them I knew we were going to get better, but I wasn't sure we'd be around coaching this team when it happened," laughed Switzer.

At that point, Johnson came up with an idea for a "Beat Colorado Party" to be held on Thursday night before their trip to Boulder. Here's the wacky part: the three coaches—Switzer, Johnson and Lacewell—decided to have their spouses dress up like men while they dressed in drag.

It was something to get their minds off of the existing pressures and have a little fun.

Jimmy Johnson. *Photo courtesy of the University of Oklahoma*

The three couples gathered at the Switzer's house—Johnson in a long evening gown and wig, Lacewell in thick makeup and a wig, and Switzer in one of his wife's dresses—and the plan was to go to every other coach's house and get them to join in the fun.

"Before the evening was over, everyone was at Chuck Fairbanks' house. Every assistant and his wife was dressed up," said Switzer. "Chuck sees us having a helluva time and he goes back and throws on a white sequin dress and lipstick all over the place. It was just what we needed to forget about football for a few hours."

But it doesn't end there.

Sometime around 2 a.m., Johnson and fellow assistant Gene Hochevar were driving home when they pulled up to the corner of Lindsey Street and Berry Road. Two rednecks leaving Opie's, a local watering hole, pulled up next to them in their pickup truck and honked, thinking they might get lucky with the lovely ladies.

Johnson rolled down his window, flipped them the bird and gave the two fellas directions on where they could go.

"The entire staff got a pretty good laugh out of that," added Switzer, who pointed out that the Sooners beat Colorado that weekend, 23-15.

The "Beat Colorado Party" and its unusual theme became an annual tradition over the next several seasons in Norman.

Unwelcome Visitor

In the waning moments of the 1977 season opener, Oklahoma blocked a late Vanderbilt field goal to preserve a 25-23 victory. As the Sooners celebrated their narrow escape on the sidelines, a Vanderbilt fan approached OU assistant coach Bobby Proctor and grabbed him by his shirt.

Fellow assistant coach Warren Harper stepped in to give Proctor some assistance, and the two tossed the Commodore supporter back into the stands. Having heard about a brief scuffle near the OU bench, security arrived moments later to make sure order had been restored.

"It was kind of crazy, because here I am with this fan tugging on me, and I'm wondering what the heck is going on. Then Warren jumps in and we practically throw the guy back over the fence," said Proctor, who had previously spent a few seasons as an assistant at Vandy prior to his coming to Norman.

"Well, I come to find out the guy's kid is playing for Vanderbilt and I actually knew him pretty well. But I certainly didn't recognize him under those circumstances. He had actually come down to congratulate us on the win."

The Rhodes Less Traveled

Recruiting can be a fragile business. One wrong word, one wrong step and the most coveted of prospects can end up playing for your rival down the road. Then again, sometimes fate steps in to rescue a recruiting visit gone awry.

Such was the case when Steve Rhodes, out of Spruce High School in Dallas, decided to make his official visit to Norman on a foggy January night in 1975. The talented wide receiver had narrowed his choices down to OU, Arkansas and Texas A&M, and he was anxious to see what the two-time defending national champion Sooners were all about.

Excited about his first-ever ride in a plane, Rhodes boarded a flight in Dallas that was scheduled to arrive around 7 p.m. But it never landed in Oklahoma City due to thickening fog. Instead, Rhodes ended up in Wichita, Kansas.

"I'm sitting there waiting for Steve's flight to arrive and suddenly they announce it's going to Wichita instead," said OU assistant coach Jerry Pettibone. "I scrambled around and finally got someone in the Wichita airport to give Steve a message with my phone number. He called me and was wondering what the heck he was going to do."

Later that night, the passengers were loaded onto a bus bound for Norman, and sometime around 1 a.m. it finally pulled into town.

"I was so worried that Steve's whole trip was ruined, but he got off the bus laughing and talking to a U.S. sailor who had just spent the last three hours explaining how much he loved OU football and how great everything in Oklahoma was," said Pettibone. "He basically recruited Steve to OU for us."

A few weeks later, Rhodes committed to the Sooners, and he eventually went on to become a four-year starter.

The Congressman

The tiny football hamlet of Eufaula, Oklahoma, had already turned out three of the greatest defensive players (the Selmon brothers) in OU history when J. C. Watts decided to sign with the Sooners in 1976.

Watts, following in the footsteps of option quarterback Thomas Lott, would eventually make Eufaula proud with his work in the wishbone. But it would first take a little extra persuading by Barry Switzer and company after Watts briefly left the team following his freshman year.

"He wanted to quit and transfer to another school because he just wasn't happy," said Switzer. "He had to wait his turn behind Thomas, and that was frustrating for him. But you have to be tolerant and try to understand what he's going through."

Once Watts decided to stick around, he demonstrated his talent for making the big play in OU's option attack. In his 25 starts, the Sooners won 22 times.

After enjoying a highly successful career in the Canadian Football League, Watts returned to Oklahoma, where he was elected to Congress.

J.C. Watts. *Photo courtesy of the University of Oklahoma*

No Exposure Isn't So Bad

During Barry Switzer's first three seasons at the Oklahoma helm, his Sooners were dubbed by *Sports Illustrated* as "the best team you'll never see."

The reason was probation. NCAA sanctions prohibited the Sooners from appearing on television from November 23, 1973 to January 1, 1976. And OU did not appear in a bowl game from December 31, 1972 until January 1, 1976.

During that period, the Sooners went 32-1-1 and won a pair of national titles.

From Obscurity to the Outland

There weren't many 6-foot-4, 260-pound players quick and agile enough to play Division-I linebacker in the mid-1970s. But that was the position Greg Roberts was slated to play when the Sooners recruited him out of Nacogdoches, Texas, in 1974.

It became clear during fall practice that Roberts had a great forward burst, but lacked the lateral speed and instincts to play linebacker. After trying him there, the OU coaching staff moved him to defensive line, still with less than impressive results.

Finally during a team meeting, coach Barry Switzer decided to send Roberts to the offensive side of the ball. It was exactly what the big man needed, as his explosive first step helped earn him All-America honors twice as a guard. And in 1978, the Sooner senior picked up the Outland Trophy, which annually goes to the top offensive lineman in the country.

Tell Us How You Really Feel

Barry Switzer always held his press conference on Tuesday, to talk about the previous weekend's game and the upcoming opponent. Members of the media would ask questions on a broad range of topics. Well, Switzer always dreaded the pre-

Kansas State week because the Wildcats were traditionally so bad that he had a hard time keeping his team focused.

Typically during the press conference, someone would ask Switzer to talk about K-State and what kind of game plan he expected to see from them. And typically, the Sooner skipper would give the same old canned comments.

During one stretch in the 1980s, OU beat the Wildcats four straight times by the combined score of 226-50. In the middle of that run, Switzer was asked at his Tuesday luncheon prior to the annual Kansas State game what he thought about the Wildcats. He paused for a moment and simply replied, "Kansas State is Kansas State. What else can I say?"

That about covers it.

Party Time

During spring football practice in 1975, the OU coaches had been pushing the team pretty hard when they decided to give the players the weekend off. Hearing the good news prior to Friday practice, Chez Evans and several of his black teammates decided to throw a big party.

They took up a collection of money and charged Evans with purchasing the food and drinks. The plan was for Evans to make up a story about being sick so he could miss practice that afternoon and set up the party with the rest of their friends.

Evans was to go to team trainer Ken Rawlinson and relay the sick story, then leave. But before he could execute his plan, assistant coach Gene Hochevar overheard everything and put his own plan into motion.

"I basically told Ken to check Chez out and find something wrong so he'd think twice about skipping practice the next time," said Hochevar.

When Evans arrived with the tale of headache and an upset stomach, Rawlinson went to work, checking his patient's temperature and everything else. After a few minutes, he explained to Evans that he was really sick and he would have to be quarantined in the infirmary.

There was nothing Evans could do. By the time he was released from the infirmary on Monday morning, his teammates figured Evans had taken the money, quit the team and left town. It took plenty of explaining on his part to get back in good graces.

"When I told Chez what I'd done, he thought that was pretty cold-blooded. But we laughed about it a lot and he never showed up sick to practice again," Hochevar added.

Hey, Cab Driver

The anticipation was excruciating. The flight from Los Angeles to Hawaii seemed like it would never end. And even when it did, there was no immediate relief.

Barry Switzer's patience was being put to the ultimate test as he hurried around the Honolulu airport trying to find the answer to the $1 million question: Who won the Associated Press football poll?

The bowl season had ended the previous evening with Switzer's Oklahoma squad sitting at home, part of the national viewing audience. The Sooners were on probation and not eligible for postseason play or votes in the UPI national poll.

The AP vote, due out that day, was the only one that mattered. Unfortunately, Switzer couldn't find anyone who had heard the news.

"I'm wandering around the airport trying to find a paper, but they were all early editions. No AP results," said Switzer, whose 11-0 Sooners were the lone undefeated team in the country.

Switzer was in town to coach the annual Hula Bowl, but his mind was on the fortunes of his boys back in Norman.

"We were undefeated and already ranked number one, but I really didn't know what the outcome [of the voting] would be after the bowl games," he said.

It had been almost two decades since Oklahoma last won a national title, but Switzer could almost taste it. He finally ran into a taxi driver who was talking football with some of his buddies—and he popped the question.

"The guy tells me Oklahoma was number one in the AP poll. So there I am standing in the airport in Honolulu celebrating our national championship with some taxi driver I didn't even know," smiled Switzer.

The Tackle

Mention those two simple words and Oklahoma fans will quickly describe the hit Sooner safety Scott Hill put on Pittsburgh's Tony Dorsett during their national showdown in 1975. While the No. 1 Sooners beat the 15th-ranked Panthers 46-10 that day, it's the flying smash Hill applied to Dorsett that people remember.

The hit came midway through the second quarter with OU holding a 20-0 lead. Pitt was facing fourth and one when Dorsett got the ball on an option right. Before he had time to think about which way to cut, Hill hurdled a blocker and buried him three yards deep in the backfield.

"It was more instinct than anything, really. I guess that's what you call reckless abandon," said Hill. "I think that play helped take the steam out of them. Dorsett was pretty much done after that and we put it away."

While Dorsett was destined to win the Heisman Trophy the following season, his afternoon in Norman was forgettable. He finished with 12 carries for 17 yards and left in the second half after linebackers Bill Dalke and Jimbo Elrod sandwiched him in the backfield again.

But it was "the tackle" that fans remember most.

"That play definitely defined my career," added Hill.

Answered Prayer

A season removed from winning its second straight national title, Oklahoma was in rebound mode as it approached the stretch run of the 1976 campaign. The Sooners had suffered consecutive losses (Oklahoma State and Colorado) for the first time since 1970 and hoped wins against Kansas State and Missouri would give them some momentum going into their showdown with Nebraska at Lincoln.

As OU prepared to take the field that November day, coach Barry Switzer gathered his team around and asked senior safety Scott Hill to deliver a word of prayer.

"God keep us all healthy and don't let the best team win," said Hill.

The answer came in the form of a 20-17 Sooner victory.

Collect Call

Greg Pruitt was long gone and Joe Washington would be headed for the NFL soon, meaning Barry Switzer's Sooners would be minus a feature back in their wishbone attack. Players like Elvis Peacock, Kenny King and Horace Ivory could fill the void in the meantime, but Switzer desperately wanted a kid named Billy Sims out of Hooks, Texas.

Despite his Class A pedigree, Sims possessed the talent to carry an entire offense, and college coaches were lining up at his door by the dozens. Switzer was at the front of the line. He got in on Sims early, and they developed a strong relationship.

The Sooners were playing Colorado during the 1974 season and well on their way to a 49-14 victory by halftime. During the intermission, knowing that Sims was listening to the game on the radio, Switzer called him at the gas station where he worked.

"He was really shocked when I called him," laughed Switzer. "I probably worked Billy harder than any recruit I ever had. I felt he was that good."

Billy Sims. *Photo courtesy of the University of Oklahoma*

Things like that call tilted the scale in Switzer's favor, and Sims signed with Oklahoma. Slowed by injuries early in his career, Sims eventually blossomed into the player everyone expected. He won the Heisman Trophy as a junior when he set a Big Eight single-season rushing record with 1,762 yards on 231 carries.

CHAPTER SIX

The 1980s

How's It Going, Dick?

DURING THE 1980 SEASON, Oklahoma was scheduled to play a rare November non-conference game against No. 6 North Carolina at Memorial Stadium. The 16th-ranked Sooners had already lost twice, to Stanford and Texas, by the time the undefeated Tar Heels hit town.

Lawrence Taylor spearheaded a UNC defense that was ranked first in the country against the run, and Amos Lawrence was one of the ACC's top tailbacks. The Tar Heels were loaded, and they fully expected to waltz into Norman and beat the Sooners.

North Carolina was going through workouts at the stadium the day before the game, and OU coach Barry Switzer walked down to introduce himself to his Tar Heel counterpart.

"I walked up to Coach Crum and said, 'Hey Denny, it's great to have you here,'" explained Switzer. "When I said that I noticed that he just stared at me, didn't smile or anything. I stood there and talked about the game, saying Denny this and Denny that. I didn't think any more about it."

Later, when Switzer retreated to the OU coaches' offices, he told his staff how quiet Coach Crum was and how unfriendly he seemed.

"I just figured he was ready to play, and I told my guys we'd better play, because North Carolina meant business," said Switzer.

Game day arrived and Switzer found himself near midfield talking to Coach Crum for a second time. OU's skipper talked about the weather and how he hoped both teams played well and no one got injured—again, without much response from Crum.

At the end of the contest, after Oklahoma had completely dismantled the Tar Heels en route to a 41-7 win, Switzer made his way over to Crum and was reaching out for the traditional postgame handshake. But instead of offering up his hand, Crum walked away saying, "The name's not Denny, it's Dick."

"I remember watching the film of that, and it showed me standing there stunned. And then I realized what I'd been doing for two days—I'd been calling him Denny the whole time," added Switzer, who had Louisville basketball coach Denny Crum on his mind. "I went upstairs and told my staff what I'd been doing and they all laughed and said, 'Don't worry, Coach, North Carolina is nothing but a basketball school anyway.'"

Man Among Boys

Asked once whom he felt was the toughest, most physically capable freshman player he remembered having at Oklahoma, Barry Switzer hesitated for a moment and offered the following:

"We've had a lot of great freshman players here, going way back to Bud Wilkinson's days, but as far as being physically and mentally tough and mature, I'd have to say Lydell Carr. He was one tough son of a bitch, a complete stallion from the day he arrived on campus."

Carr, from Enid, Oklahoma, was pure muscle from head to toe, cut like an anvil from the waist up. He started each of his four years at fullback for Switzer's Sooners from 1984-87.

Illegal Procedure and the Ponies

Oklahoma fans will probably never forget the untimely trip the Sooner Schooner made during the 1985 Orange Bowl. It wound up costing the Sooners three points and possibly a victory over PAC-10 power Washington.

"The whole thing was just strange, the way it all played out," said OU kicker Tim Lashar.

With the game tied 14-14 early in the fourth quarter, the Sooners lined up for what promised to be a go-ahead 22-yard field goal. But here's the twist: OU lineman Mark Hutson was checking in and out of the game wearing jerseys 79 and 90, depending on whether he lined up on the interior or at tight end. Every time he entered the game with a different number, he was required to check in with officials. But he failed to do so on the field goal attempt.

Lashar easily hit the short field goal, but officials flagged Hutson for illegal substitution.

"They threw the flag into the middle of the line, so nobody saw it. We all ran to the sideline thinking the kick was good, and the Schooner made its run onto the field like it did every time we scored," explained Lashar.

By the time the Sooners realized they had to replay the down, the officials had tacked a 15-yard penalty on the Schooner for coming onto the field. Lashar wound up trying a 42-yard field goal that Washington blocked.

"I think that deflated us to a point, but we still managed to come back and take a 17-14 lead," added Lashar. "Unfortunately, the wheels pretty much came off for us after that, and Washington really played well the last few minutes."

Washington won the contest 28-17, canceling any planned celebration in the stables that night.

Big Marcus

Described by Barry Switzer as "the most talented player, the most hyped player the University of Oklahoma ever recruited," Marcus Dupree fashioned his legend as a Sooner in a total of 17 games.

The Philadelphia, Mississippi, product was a special blend of power and speed. His 230-pound frame covered ground like a runaway freight train, and he flourished in the latter part of his freshman season after OU switched from the wishbone to the I formation.

"When you talk about pure running talent, making people miss, stopping and starting, stepping sideways—Marcus Dupree could do it all," said Barry Switzer.

But after capping his rookie year with a 246-yard rushing performance in the 1983 Fiesta Bowl, Dupree began struggling with his weight and was still struggling to adjust to college life. Just five games into his sophomore season, after being held to 50 yards in a loss to Texas, he returned home to Mississippi and never played another game for the Sooners.

"He might have been the best ever. But we'll never know," said Switzer. "It will always be the untold story, and that's a shame."

Live Wire

For years, Howard Newman was the man behind the OU coach's television show. He was always coming up with ideas to make the show more interesting and one week he decided to "mic" an OU assistant coach in order to give fans a feel for what goes on on the sideline during a game.

After some debate, Newman agreed that longtime Barry Switzer staffer Bobby Proctor would be their man. During pregame, they wired Proctor for sound and then sent him boldly into the fray.

Fortunately, Proctor wasn't being broadcast live that day as the Sooners battled Kansas State in Manhattan. By the time the Sooners dashed back into the halftime locker room they were trailing 18-3, and Proctor had used every expletive in the book.

"Nothing I said seemed to light a fire under us, so I had to break out a few bad words," admitted Proctor. "I saw Howard standing over to the side and I told him they needed to take the wire off of me because to that point I hadn't given them a single word they could use. And I wasn't sure if it was going to get any better in the second half."

Newman talked the coach into keeping the wire on, and it turned out just fine, as the Sooners rallied to win 28-21.

Hot Water Cornbread

Oklahoma had switched from the wishbone to the I formation prior to the 1982 season, and it looked as if Barry Switzer was expanding his offensive philosophy to include more of an aerial game. When the 1983 recruiting season kicked in, pass catchers were critical to Switzer's want list.

Keith Jackson was at the top of that list.

"I remember when Coach Switzer walked in the door at our house and sat down on the couch. I was thinking we were about to hear all of this football gibberish, and instead he leaned back and said, 'Gladys, can you make hot water cornbread?'" described Jackson. "He and my mother carried on about hot water cornbread, beans and greens, and never talked about football once."

The Jacksons quickly warmed to Switzer, and he made himself comfortable by slipping off his shoes while he sat back and talked about life.

"My mother looked at Coach Switzer and said, 'Now that's the first time a white man has ever taken his shoes off in my house,'" laughed Jackson. "It was very interesting because he sold the type of man he was. He sold his heart to my mother. She had really wanted me to go to Arkansas, but she told me if

I decided to go anywhere else, Oklahoma is where she wanted me to go."

When Jackson made his visit to Norman, he said it was the players who really sold him on the program. He described the team and the campus as having a family atmosphere.

"That's what separates Oklahoma from a lot of other schools. The guys here get along and watch out for one another," added Jackson.

Jackson eventually based his decision on the fact that OU was recruiting a passing quarterback from Henryetta, Oklahoma, by the name of Troy Aikman. The Sooners had been passing more during the early 1980s and Jackson figured that trend might continue.

Aikman's OU career ended in 1985 due to a broken leg, and Jackson wound up catching a total of 62 passes for his entire career. That was still good enough to earn him All-America honors twice.

Head-On Collision

What happens when a pair of 280-pound linemen running at full speed crash into each other? Headaches, that's what. Anthony Phillips and Mark Hudson can attest to that.

The two-time All-Americans experienced just such a crash during a third-quarter play in the 1985 Nebraska game. Leading 14-0 and driving inside the Cornhusker 20, Oklahoma called a sweep play that called for a pulling guard to clear the way with a lead block. The only problem was, Phillips and Hudson each believed they were the one supposed to pull.

"It was a violent collision," said Merv Johnson, OU offensive line coach at the time. "Both pulled and ran face up into each other. They play-busted and almost cost us the drive, but worse, it almost knocked both of those guys out. I'm not going to say which one was wrong, but it was a pretty ugly scene for a moment."

Play was stopped while the two mammoth linemen slowly got to their feet and tried to ready themselves for the next snap. Finally, OU was forced to call a timeout.

"They were cussing each other out and staggering around. It wasn't funny, but under different circumstances it could have been," smiled Johnson. "Once they shook the cobwebs out, they went back in and we eventually scored to put the game away."

Good Advice

When Keith Jackson was being recruited by Oklahoma, running back Spencer Tillman served as his host for the weekend. The two became fast friends and would eventually play three seasons together for the Sooners.

Jackson, who became known for his flare for dramatics, confronted Tillman about a certain play he had been involved in against Nebraska the previous season.

"I told him I saw him in that Nebraska game when you jumped over those defenders to get into the end zone. I said, 'You could have stopped and gone around them just as easily,'" offered Jackson. "And he told me great players make great plays at great times. That stuck with me for the rest of my career."

A Player's Coach

No one will argue that Barry Switzer wasn't, at times, viewed as a cocky SOB who knew how to push people's buttons and get into an opposing coach's head. He said what was on his mind and occasionally did things that landed him in hot water.

That's his way.

But on the flip side, Switzer could not have been more popular with his players. He cared for his athletes and treated them like family. He believed in second chances. In turn, they did not hesitate to go to war with him every Saturday.

"I tell people any day and every day that Barry Switzer is a person I will idolize for the rest of my life," said running back Earl Johnson. "In my mind, there is nothing you can say bad about Coach Switzer. He was a player's coach—[the players] were his primary concern and he made sure we knew that."

A Higher Power

During his playing days at Oklahoma, Lucious Selmon could rely heavily on his physical skills to help him succeed in almost any situation. Privately, he was a spiritual man. But on the field, he controlled his own destiny along with his teammates.

Destiny was no longer directly in his hands after he became an assistant coach on Barry Switzer's staff. And that took a little getting used to for the former All-American nose guard.

During the 1986 OU-Nebraska game in Lincoln, as the Sooners rallied behind an unforgettable performance from tight end Keith Jackson, fellow assistant coach Bobby Proctor noticed Selmon kneeling at the opposite end of the bench from where the action was taking place.

In the moments after Jackson had stunned the crowd with a beautiful catch that helped seal a 20-17 OU victory, Proctor asked Selmon what he was doing all bent over and avoiding the watching.

"Praying," Selmon said.

Maybe "Sooner Magic" was simply a matter of divine intervention?

Not a Big Baseball Fan?

During a practice session prior to the 1989 Citrus Bowl in Orlando, Oklahoma had just finished up drills when OU sports information director Mike Treps approached Barry Switzer. Treps pointed to the sideline and told the Sooner coach that Tim Raines would like to meet him.

Switzer's response: "Who the heck is Tim Raines?"

Treps explained that Raines played for the Montreal Expos and was considered one of the best players in the National League at the time. Hearing that, Switzer walked over to Raines, smiled and warmly stated, "Tim, it's really great to meet you. I think you're a great player."

Fresh Squeezed

Nine times during Barry Switzer's 16 seasons as head coach, Oklahoma went to the Orange Bowl as Big Eight champs. Sooner fans became regulars at South Beach in Miami, and their team usually gave them something to celebrate, winning six times.

As OU's trips to the Sunshine State became regular, so did the fans' propensity to throw oranges onto Owen Field as a sign of their support. Although OU officials outlawed the flying fruit, that didn't stop overly enthusiastic fans from sharing their best Nolan Ryan impersonation.

"When we were in the hunt, which was pretty much always, every time we scored a touchdown you knew what was coming from the stands," said All-America tight end Keith Jackson. "You made sure you kept your helmet on when the oranges started flying. An orange that is thrown from several rows up could really hurt."

The Sooners were playing Nebraska in the regular-season finale in 1987, with the winner set to claim the conference title and earn a trip to Miami. The showdown was billed as the "Game of the Century II," after the Huskers had replaced the Sooners as the top-ranked team in the country earlier that week.

There were plenty of pockets stuffed with oranges, but Nebraska made sure the flight patterns were clear during the opening half by taking a 7-0 lead into the locker room. That, however, would change over the final 30 minutes as Anthony Stafford and Patrick Collins gave the Sooners the lead with a pair of touchdown runs.

"I remember the first time we scored, everyone was excited and here come the oranges flying. Everybody on the sideline was saying, 'Put your helmets on, put your helmets on,'" said Jackson.

Coach Charlie North watched several citrus projectiles zip overhead, and he turned around to tell the fans to stop throwing oranges. Well, a few minutes later Collins snapped off a 65-yard scoring run, and the place went wild with oranges flying in every direction.

"Someone threw an orange and it traveled a long way before hitting Coach North in the head. At the time, you wanted to make sure he was OK, but once you knew that, it was hilarious," laughed Jackson. "After that, he didn't worry about telling people not to throw oranges. He took cover like everyone else."

With or Without Troy

If 1984 was disappointing to Sooner fans, then 1985 held all the hope of a potential championship season. OU returned plenty of talent on both sides of the ball, including the nucleus of one of the best defenses in the country and all the makings of a powerful offensive attack.

Brian Bosworth, Keith Jackson, Kevin Murphy, Tony Casillas, Rickey Dixon, Darrell Reed and Danté Jones were just a few of the marquee names that highlighted a star-studded Sooner lineup. The one ingredient in question was quarterback.

Troy Aikman, a 6-foot-4 sophomore, hoped to provide any and all answers with his big arm and talented supporting cast. But Aikman's career as a starting quarterback lasted only four games. He suffered a broken leg in a 27-14 loss to Miami and would never play again for the Sooners.

"I don't want to say it was a blessing that Troy got hurt, but I'm not sure we could have done the things we did the rest of that season with him at quarterback," said Bosworth, OU's outspoken All-America linebacker. "I think the talent we had on

Troy Aikman. *Photo courtesy of the University of Oklahoma*

offense certainly flourished more under Jamelle [Holieway]. He was better-suited for that offense."

What OU did that season, with a 17-year-old freshman under center, was nothing short of amazing. Barry Switzer's squad reeled off eight straight wins after the loss to Miami, including a 25-10 national title-clinching victory over Penn State in the Orange Bowl.

"Coach Switzer had a lot of confidence in Jamelle, and Jamelle had a lot of confidence and wisdom beyond his age," offered All-America tight end Keith Jackson. "He understood football. He ran the wishbone at Bannon High School, and when he stepped out on the field that season, he was just like a senior. Jamelle came from that neighborhood where he had that attitude 'Nobody's tougher than I am.'

"He was a special player and that was a special team."

Dominating Defense

Still smarting from the sting of a 15-15 tie in Dallas the previous season (a game replays showed they were robbed of), Oklahoma had just a bit of red-ass going when it stepped onto the Cotton Bowl turf to meet Texas in 1985.

The second-ranked Sooners were anxious to take their angst out on the Longhorns, but they would have to do it without the services of injured All-America nose guard Tony Casillas. That turned out to be no problem for the Brian Bosworth and Kevin Murphy-led defense, which held Texas to four first downs and 70 total yards.

"It was one of the most dominating performances I'd seen, especially to do it without one of your best players. That says a lot," said OU coach Barry Switzer. "The score really didn't reflect how badly we kicked their butts that day."

OU actually trailed 7-0 after Texas returned a first-quarter fumble for a score. But thanks to their defense, the Sooners rallied past the frustrated Horns and finally took the lead on an option pitch from Troy Aikman to Patrick Collins that covered 45 yards in the fourth quarter.

"The way the 1984 game finished planted the seed for the next season," said Bosworth, a two-time Butkus Award winner. "I had so much hatred in my gut for Texas, I just wanted to go out and kick them. From the very first whistle to the very end, I didn't want to do anything other than make every single play a domination of the Texas Longhorns."

Mission accomplished.

Double the Magic

While Barry Switzer always pointed out that "Sooner Magic" came into existence during the OU-Nebraska series, it was not reserved only for the Huskers. During the 1980 season, the Sooners used it on Nebraska and then saved a little for Orange Bowl foe Florida State.

The result was a pair of last-minute victories over Tom Osborne and Bobby Bowden.

Nebraska fans were gearing up for celebration with just over three minutes left when freshman Buster Rhymes broke loose on a 43-yard option run that set up more late-game heroics. A 13-yard pass from J. C. Watts to Bobby Grayson set up a one-yard touchdown run by Rhymes, thus producing a 21-17 OU victory.

The Sooners beat Oklahoma State 63-17 the following week and then pulled out the magic again on January 1, 1981, against the Seminoles.

"It wasn't something you could predict. It just happened, and when it did, it was special," said Switzer, describing the phenomena known as "Sooner Magic."

Oklahoma had beaten Florida State 24-7 in the Orange Bowl a year earlier, but the Seminoles grabbed a 17-10 lead in the rematch thanks to an OU fumble they recovered for a touchdown.

OU vs. Nebraska. *Photo courtesy of the University of Oklahoma*

Watts was at his best in the final three minutes as he marched the Sooners, using a surprisingly effective passing game, inside the FSU 20. A 42-yard strike to Steve Rhodes set up the drama, and Watts went back to Rhodes for an 11-yard TD with just 1:27 remaining. The Sooners capped the comeback when Watts, the game's MVP, found Forrest Valora in the end zone for the deciding two-point conversion.

Intimidation or Entertainment

Brian Bosworth, aka "The Boz," was notorious for his on-the-field conversations with opposing players. No one talked more smack than Bosworth and no one backed it up better, either.

The best moment of every game, according to defensive back Sonny Brown, was when Bosworth recorded his first tackle. That's when he really opened up the vocabulary and let the remarks fly.

"I'd run all the way across the field just to listen to him talk crap on the guy he hit," laughed Brown. "It was hilarious. You could just see the running back's eyes getting bigger and the fear creeping in.

"Brian used it more for the intimidation factor, but for the rest of us, it was more about entertainment."

Collins and Stafford

So many great running backs have graced the backfields of so many fine Oklahoma teams, it's easy to forget some of the guys who maybe didn't have the marquee name or flashy credentials. Barry Switzer can recite an entire roster of players whom he deems every bit as critical to the Sooners' overall success as some of the All-Americans.

Two of those "underrated" heroes were Patrick Collins and Anthony Stafford, who formed a formidable tag team in Switzer's backfield for three seasons. Although neither player's name appears among the Sooners' all-time rushing leaders, their contributions helped OU compile an incredible 33-3 record from 1985-87.

"Those guys were really good players because they were intelligent, they never made mistakes and they were great blockers. Plus, they really executed well in our option game," said Switzer. "It was neat to have Patrick and Anthony together for three years like that, because I never had to worry about them. They were so unselfish, they didn't care about how many times they carried or how many yards they made.

"They just wanted to win. I'd take a hundred more just like them."

Bad Timing

Oklahoma seemingly always had an abundance of talent during Barry Switzer's 16 seasons as head coach. The depth chart often resembled a Who's Who of high school standouts, many of whom were caught up in the numbers game and never got to realize their potential at the Division I level.

One player who had all of the talent in the world was Eric Mitchel. One of the most sought-after prep quarterbacks in the country in 1984, Mitchel joined the Sooners basically at the same time as Troy Aikman and Jamelle Holieway. He was a product of bad timing.

Mitchel battled valiantly for the starting job each of his four years at Oklahoma, coming up just short each time. When he did see the field he demonstrated flashes of brilliance, producing five 100-yard rushing games in a backup role.

The most amazing stat from Mitchel's career came from his performances against Big Eight rival Kansas State. In three games against the Wildcats, Mitchel carried the ball 25 times for 436 yards. That's 17.4 yards per carry.

In the 1987 contest, Mitchel went for 149 yards on seven touches. The following season, he carried six times for 161 yards.

Unfortunately, he could never quite nudge Holieway out of the starting QB spot. Still, many people believe the Sooners would have been in very capable hands if the roles were reversed.

The Boz Is Born

Growing up an Oklahoma football fan in the heart of Texas forged Brian Bosworth into a young man who felt destined for something special. He lived for Saturdays and listening to or watching the Sooners work their magic, and he knew that some day he would be a part of it.

Those visions, if you will, came to pass when the lightly recruited Bosworth signed with Barry Switzer's program. From the moment he walked on that campus, his confident style made him stand out. And he expeditiously used his speed, strength and instincts to become a budding superstar.

But something was missing. Bosworth needed a means of channeling all of his talent, emotions and complexity into his

Brian Bosworth. *Photo courtesy of the University of Oklahoma*

game. The 1984 OU-Texas game presented him with that outlet. His name was the Boz.

"I had looked forward to that first OU-Texas game from the time I was six years old. Being from Oklahoma and having to move to Texas, I was really the only kid I knew who rooted for OU in Texas," said Bosworth. "That first game was really the birth of my alter ego, the ability for me to go in and find an area inside myself of pure intensity. That enabled me to elevate my game to another level—which really is the definition of the OU-Texas game."

During his three seasons (1984-86) at Oklahoma, Bosworth matured into one of the greatest linebackers in college football history. He also created a character that was both loved and loathed. And too often the lines became blurred between the football player and the character.

Bosworth was a model student who earned Academic All-America honors. He worked diligently on his business degree and made friends at the drop of a hat. The Boz was bold, brash and borderline arrogant. He was known for fashionable hairstyles, colorful comments and outrageous exploits.

"Boz was a gifted college football player. He had great speed and an attitude that made him special," said teammate Keith Jackson. "A lot of people only saw the haircut and the antics and looked at him as if he was some kind of commando out there. But he really was a leader and a very smart football player.

"Bosworth understood defense probably as well as [OU defensive coordinator] Gary Gibbs did. He knew how to play the game and he made a habit of making great plays. Boz was a football player—bottom line."

To Onside Kick or Not to Onside Kick

There are plenty of legendary stories that define Oklahoma's domination of Oklahoma State in the Bedlam series. But few can top the craziness of the 1983 battle in Stillwater.

Fast-forward to the final 10 minutes of the game. The Cowboys own a 20-3 lead and celebrations have already started breaking out in the stands at Lewis Field. But OSU fans should have realized this one is far from over.

The Sooners got themselves back into the game on a short flat pass that Derrick Shepard turned into a 73-yard touchdown reception. Tim Lashar's point-after kick cut the lead to 20-10 with just under nine minutes remaining. Two possessions later, Spencer Tillman capped another OU scoring drive with a short

Bosworth vs. Texas. *Photo courtesy of the University of Oklahoma*

run. And when quarterback Danny Bradley hit Earl Johnson with a perfect two-point conversion pass, the Sooners trailed 20-18 with just under two minutes left.

That's when the real fun began.

Coach Barry Switzer and his staff discussed their options on the sideline in the ensuing moments, and there was some confusion as to whether or not they were going to attempt an onside kick or not.

"I heard Coach Switzer come over and say we want to go ahead and kick it deep, but no one ever gave me a definitive answer," explained Lashar. "All I hear is [coach] Bobby Proctor saying we need to get the ball back."

To make certain everyone is on the same page, coverage man Dwight Drane runs up and down the 30-yard line informing his teammates about the decision to kick deep. But Lashar is teeing up the ball 10 yards away, out of earshot and unaware of Drane's message.

"I never heard him, so I'm still thinking we're going with the onside," admitted Lashar, who proceeded to kick a line-drive knuckler that bounced off the facemask of OSU's Chris Rockins.

The ball ricocheted straight to OU's Scott Case, who had the presence of mind to grab it and run directly out of bounds near midfield. Several plays later, Lashar booted the game-winning 46-yard field goal with 1:14 left.

"Some times it's better to be lucky than good," smiled Lashar.

OU 21, OSU 20.

Head Games

The Oklahoma-Nebraska series always produces big hits, big plays and unusual moments. David Vickers experienced all of the above in a single moment during the 1986 affair in Lincoln.

After making a bone-crunching tackle on a running play near the OU sideline, Vickers jogged back to join his teammates in the huddle. Once there, the defensive back began banging his hand against his head, repeatedly.

"I looked over and wondered what the heck he was doing and he says, 'I can't feel my head,'" said teammate Sonny Brown. "The hit had left his entire head numb, so we got him out of the game pretty fast. It wasn't very funny at the time, but we laughed about it later."

What If?

To borrow a line from Mark Twain, "The rumors of my demise are greatly exaggerated." That must have been what Mike Gaddis was thinking as he returned to action in 1991 after missing parts of two seasons with a career-threatening knee injury.

The media had all but written the Oklahoma running back off after he suffered a torn anterior cruciate ligament in his left knee during third-quarter action of the OU-Texas game in 1989. At least 14 long months of rehabilitation awaited Gaddis, and then there was the psychological toll the injury might take.

A successful comeback was not realistic, many believed.

"I heard all of the rumors," admitted Gaddis. "I knew it would be a long road back, but I was determined to get there. I didn't want my college football career to end like that. I wanted to do more."

A week before hurting his knee, Gaddis had stepped into the spotlight with a phenomenal 274-yard rushing effort in a 37-15 win over Oklahoma State. Just a sophomore, he was on the verge of becoming a Heisman Trophy candidate at the ripe old age of 19.

"I always said Mike Gaddis was the best running back ever recruited out of the state of Oklahoma," said Barry Switzer. "If he stays healthy, he's a top-five draft in the NFL. As it was, he still had a fine career, thanks to lots of courage."

When the Carl Albert product returned in '91, he quickly silenced any and all doubters with one extraordinary performance after another. During a three-game stretch late in the season, Gaddis ran for 191, 217 and 203 yards against Kansas State, Missouri and OSU.

How's the Weather Up There?

It seems the Bedlam series always provides at least one or two twists of fate or unusual circumstances, and the 1985 version of OU and Oklahoma State's annual war certainly did not disappoint.

The game, originally scheduled for a 1:30 p.m. kickoff, was changed to a night game to accommodate ESPN and a national television audience. As it turned out, much of that Saturday was a bit on the chilly side, but the 11th-hour forecast called for freezing temperatures, and worse, possible snow.

Coach Barry Switzer was already unhappy with the decision to move a late November game to night, but he was about to get a whole lot unhappier. By kickoff, an ice storm was raging across the state, and Stillwater was directly in its path. Conditions at Lewis Field worsened by the minute as the sheet of sleet covering the field grew thicker and thicker.

"It was ridiculous, like an ice rink out there. We were worried about getting people hurt and freezing to death at the same time," said Switzer, whose team skated its way to a 10-0 halftime lead. "In all my years of coaching, those were the worst conditions I ever saw."

The Ice Bowl, as it became known, featured single-digit temperatures and very little offense from either team. OU's Brian Bosworth and Tony Casillas-led defense surrendered only 131 total yards to an OSU team ranked 17th in the country.

Moments before Tim Lashar's second field goal made it a 13-0 game, OU quarterback Jamelle Holieway called time out and slid his way over to Switzer on the sideline.

"Coach, you lied to me," were the first words out of Holieway's mouth. "You told me if I came to school at Oklahoma I'd never have to play in weather like this."

Switzer wasted little time with his reply: "I didn't lie to you, you dumbass. I've never seen weather like this in my life. I certainly never expected to play in this stuff, and if we would have played the game earlier when we were supposed to, we wouldn't be having this conversation right now."

The third-ranked Sooners went on to win that night to keep their national championship hopes alive. And a little over a

Barry Switzer. *Photo courtesy of the University of Oklahoma*

month later, in the warm Miami sunshine, Holieway and company beat Penn State to earn the title.

Red River Rhetoric

Fans in need of a reminder why the Oklahoma-Texas series has always been so intense and so memorable could always count on Brian Bosworth to refresh their fleeting memories. The Boz, as he was known during his playing days at Oklahoma from 1984-86, defined it as follows:

"It's David versus Goliath. It's good versus evil. It's the intense history of the two rival institutions. You throw all of the statistics out when OU and Texas play. There are no number ones and no number twos; it's simply a game between two teams who I believe really hate each other. That's one of the main reasons why these kids go to these schools, and I think from that standpoint, you're never going to find a better rivalry."

Life Saver

Oklahoma running back Spencer Tillman discovered during his rookie season in the NFL that special teams players get all the tough assignments. But he never realized how easy he had it until the afternoon of October 25, 1987.

Houston was scheduled to play Atlanta that day, and on his way to the Astrodome, Tillman warmed up in a most unusual way. As the cab he was in made its way toward the stadium on a local freeway, the driver collapsed, forcing Tillman to somehow take control of the cab and get it out of traffic.

Stranded on the side of the road, Tillman administered CPR on the driver, saving his life.

Houston beat Atlanta that afternoon, 37-33.

Knock, Knock

After lying unconscious for several minutes as a result of a head-on collision with a Baylor player, linebacker Paul Migliazzo stumbled to his feet and slowly made his way to the sideline with the help of his teammates. It was the third quarter, and OU was well on its way to a 34-15 victory over the Bears.

Much of the afternoon became little more than a blur for Migliazzo.

"They said I was standing on the sideline answering questions and talking to my teammates, but I couldn't tell you a single word I said," recalled Migliazzo. "I did remember scoring a touchdown on an interception in the first half, but everything else from that point to when I got knocked out was fuzzy."

When Migliazzo's head finally cleared in the fourth quarter, his teammates decided to have a little fun with him. Mike Mantle, Sonny Brown and Evan Gatewood began embellishing on Migliazzo's performance, describing the "other" TD he scored via a fumble and how he was unbelievable while in his punch-drunken state.

"Paul was all smiles. We had him believing he had three interceptions and had done all of this other stuff. That was funny," said Brown, a defensive back from Alice, Texas.

"I was feeling pretty good about myself," said Migliazzo. "Then I see them laughing and I come to find out they were just yanking my chain the whole time."

CHAPTER SEVEN

The 1990s and Beyond

Sweet Redemption

FOOTBALL HEROES WERE HARDER TO COME BY in the 1990s, as the Sooners struggled through one of the worst periods in their illustrious history. James Allen, a much-ballyhooed and later oft-criticized running back, earned his hero status. But it took some overtime work to get it done.

Allen experienced the high point of his career against OU's archrival Texas, as well as the low point. There was no middle ground, or so it seemed.

The high point came in the 1996 Red River showdown in Dallas. The Sooners staged a furious rally in the final six minutes of the contest, using a 51-yard punt return for touchdown by Jarrail Jackson and a 44-yard field goal from Jeremy Alexander with 2:26 remaining to send the game into overtime.

Two seasons earlier, the Sooners were in position to possibly win or tie the Longhorns when Allen was stopped a yard shy of the end zone on a fourth-and-goal play in the game's final minute. OU lost that day, 17-10.

"I'm not going to say it wasn't going through my mind when we started driving in overtime. It was," admitted Allen. "In that situation, every player wants the ball."

Texas had taken a 27-24 lead in the extra session, setting up the Sooners' late-game heroics. They drove to the Horns' two, and Allen got the call from there. Touchdown.

Coach John Blake's OU squad, which entered the game with an 0-4 record, was a 22-point underdog against the 25th-ranked Horns.

A Crooner for the Sooners

Singer-songwriter Toby Keith, a longtime Oklahoma football fan, got his chance to rub shoulder pads with some crimson and cream heroes when he participated in OU's 1994 Red-White football game. A semi pro football player prior to his successful career in country music, Keith asked the school's athletic department if he might be allowed to "get in a few moments of action" at the annual event.

Entertainment Tonight caught it all on film. But as it turned out, Keith, a native of nearby Moore, may have wished he had stayed on the sidelines as a spectator. Inserted as a defensive line replacement on the game's final series, it took all of two snaps before Keith got his leg caught under another player and suffered a broken ankle.

After leaving the scene in an ambulance, Keith was forced to cancel a concert scheduled for Tulsa later that night. And while he has remained a loyal OU supporter, he's limited his game activities to the sidelines.

The Great Crash

October 16, 1993, began like so many Saturdays before in Norman, with Oklahoma's football team on a roll at 5-0 and fresh off of a 38-17 whipping of Texas. The ninth-ranked

Sooners were set to host No. 20 Colorado in front of 64,000 strong at Memorial Stadium.

Gary Gibbs' program had finally found a groove, and there was actual talk of winning the national title again. But those thoughts were buried that afternoon under an avalanche of misfortune.

The first sign that it wasn't going to be the hosts' day occurred in the second quarter after OU took a 7-0 lead. The Sooner Schooner turned over as it raced around Owen Field celebrating the score.

It was believed that a restraining piece of the Conestoga between the two ponies—Boomer and Sooner—came loose, allowing the Schooner to jack knife and roll onto its right side. The crash left the horses unharmed, but driver Scott Gibson broke his leg in three places and passenger Ryan Ray suffered facial lacerations. Fortunately, RUF/NEKS queen Jean Connel and passenger Eric Gee endured only bruises.

The force of the wagon rolling over ripped up a huge chunk of artificial turf that had to be repaired with several strips of silver duct tape.

Things got worse in the fourth quarter when OU quarterback Cale Gundy was forced to leave after suffering a concussion as a result of his helmet bouncing off the turf. Any hopes for victory exited at that moment.

Colorado went on to win 27-10. The Sooners lost two more times in '93, and Oklahoma replaced the old artificial turf with natural grass prior to the 1994 campaign.

How Many Fingers?

Oklahoma had been working on hand signals with its defensive backs, pointing out various formations and coverages that arose on the fly. Problem was, starting safety Jason Belser kept forgetting the signals during games, or he would forget to look over and pick up the sign.

The Sooners were playing Kansas in 1990, and the Jayhawks had come into the contest with a fairly succesful passing game intact. OU assistant Bobby Proctor did his best all week to make sure Belser was well versed in all of the coverage signs.

"I'd point at my eye, which meant 'read,' and then I'd point at my tail, which meant 'read the tight end,'" recalled Proctor.

During the game, Proctor kept giving Belser various signs, but the Sooner junior was having trouble picking them up, so he simply ignored his coach. Proctor would remind him after every series, and the two-time All-Big Eight defender never responded.

Finally, after KU had completed a couple of passes to the tight end, Proctor screamed out to look for the sign. Belser's response was to shoot his coach the bird, which Proctor returned without hesitation.

"Jason came over after the play and said, 'I can't believe you'd give me the finger like that, Coach,'" added Proctor. "And I told him I was glad that I finally found a sign that he understood."

Leave it to Beavers

There were a few seasons during the decade of the '90s when finding positives and something to smile about was a bit of a challenge for Oklahoma football players and fans. That was never a problem for Aubrey Beavers, whose sense of humor was a saving grace at times.

Beavers, a talented linebacker who ended up being a second-round NFL draft pick by Miami, managed to keep the locker room atmosphere light with an endless array of pranks and practical jokes.

"Besides being a fantastic football player, Aubrey was always the team clown. He loved to talk. He also loved his people and if you were a part of the team, you were part of his family," said quarterback Cale Gundy, who played with Beavers from 1992-93.

One of Beavers' most famous quotes came after the Sooners ended up in 15-15 tie with Bedlam rival Oklahoma State in 1992.

"This feels so bad," Beavers said. "Finishing tied with OSU isn't like kissing your sister, it's like kissing your ugly twin sisters."

The Walk

There were very few positives about Howard Schnellenberger's lone season as OU's head coach. The pipe-smoking, brash-talking skipper did install one short-lived tradition that Sooner fans loved—The Walk.

On Saturdays before every home game, Schnellenberger would have his team parade through campus, starting at Sooner House and finishing at Memorial Stadium. Spectators often lined the way and it proved to be a good way of building unity with their fan base.

OU's Number-One Fan

From 1952 to 1994, Oklahoma football was Cecil Samara's passion. And during that time, the Oklahoma City native was known as OU's number-one fan, along with his famous 1923 Model T Ford, which was a staple at Sooner home games.

As the story goes, Samara was angered by a 1952 article in *True Magazine* that stated the only reason Bud Wilkinson's OU football program was a success was because Oklahoma's 700 millionaires paid for it. At the time, Samara had been given an old Model T as payment on a debt, and he decided to make the most of the compensation.

"We had an uncle who tinkered with cars, and he and my father began working on the Model T to get it running again," explained Samara's daughter, Sissy Tubb. "When they were done, they decided to drive it to Dallas for the OU-Texas game, and they put a sign made out of cardboard in the window that read: 'Sponsored by Oklahoma's 700 millionaires.' Well, people got the joke."

Samara and the car became regulars from that day on, including countless trips to Dallas for the Red River Rivalry and six trips to the Orange Bowl. Samara continued to refurbish the car over the years, and it eventually became known as "Big Red Rocket."

During games, Samara would hang out on the sidelines with the OU RUF/NEKS, the spirit group that continues to maintain the Rocket to this day. His raspy voice would carry into the stands at the north end of Memorial Stadium, "Score defense, score," or "Orange Bowl. Orange Bowl."

"Cecil wasn't just part of OU tradition, he became kind of a cult icon," said Clarke Stroud, who served as a RUF/NEK from 1987-90. "He was a great friend of the RUF/NEKS, an amazing man, very kind, very generous. And what a great Sooner fan. He certainly left a legacy."

Even though Samara passed away in July 1994 at age 79, the tradition he started lives on.

Survey Says

There has always been a small group of people whose main goal in life is to move the annual Oklahoma-Texas rivalry away from Dallas. Make it a home-and-home series in an effort to bring more revenue to the school's respective campuses and towns.

Forces opposing such a change are strong and unyielding. And in a 1994 survey of some 4,400 OU students and season ticket holders, the answer to the question was clear. Just over 81 percent of those who answered the survey preferred the game's traditional site—the Cotton Bowl in Dallas.

Nice Finish

A promising 5-0 start had fizzled thanks to three hard-fought conference losses in 1993. It was Gary Gibbs' fifth year at the helm, and the ninth-ranked Sooners were briefly back in the national picture for the first time since 1987.

A loss to Nebraska closed out the regular season and earned the Sooners an invitation to the John Hancock Bowl in El Paso, Texas. One of the top six bowls that season, but not exactly stocked with the same appeal the Orange Bowl carries.

And to top it off, OU was slated to face an unranked Texas Tech squad that only got the bid because of its close proximity to the venue. Much of the talk going into the game centered around Tech running back Bam Morris and his talents.

But by the end of that Christmas Eve showdown, Morris had been overshadowed by OU quarterback Cale Gundy in an impressive 41-10 thrashing.

"We had hopes of going to the Orange Bowl and winning the Big Eight championship that season, but it just didn't work out that way," said Gundy. "But we were determined to play well and we did. The defense shutdown Bam Morris, and we had a very good day offensively."

Gundy completed 15 of 26 passes that night for 215 yards and three touchdowns, two of which went to tight end Rickey Brady. The Sooners rolled out to a 28-3 lead by the intermission and never looked back.

"It was a good way to go out and finish my career," added Gundy, who finished as OU's all-time leader in just about every statistical passing category.

The Softer Side

Howard Schnellenberger left little in the way of a lasting legacy when he resigned under pressure from OU president David Boren after just one season. There were rumors of excessive drinking and outrageous conduct away from the field.

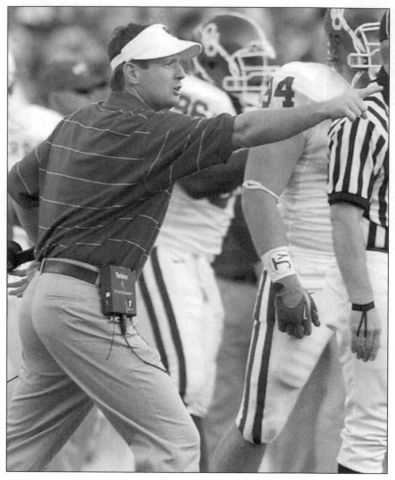

Bob Stoops. *Photo by Jerry Laizure*

And his lack of respect for the tradition that came before made him few friends of Sooners past.

But Schnellenberger wasn't all bad.

A few months into his stint as OU coach, Schnelly and his wife were invited over to a neighborhood party where everyone basically spent the evening getting to know each other. After all of the guests had arrived and gathered in the family room, the hosts had every individual stand up, make introductions and share a little something about their lives.

One elderly gentleman who was recovering from a stroke struggled to keep his balance as he got up from his chair. Seeing the situation, Schnellenberger joined the man in standing and helped steady him by holding his arm.

"I've got you, big fella," said Schnellenberger in a gruff but calming voice. "I'll take care of the balance part if you'll take care of the story."

It was a touching scene.

Bob Who?

Outside of coaching circles, Bob Stoops was not exactly a household name in 1998. Sure, he had developed into one of the top defensive coordinators in the country, but that did not guarantee him much in the way of public notoriety (at least outside Florida, where he was coaching at the time).

But even though college football fans may not have been aware of Stoops' impressive credentials, Joe Castiglione knew all he needed to know about the man. And when it came time to hire a new football coach, OU's athletic director went straight for Stoops.

"I was aware of Bob's career from its earliest stages. I kept an eye on him long before he was an assistant at Florida," said Castiglione. "Everything he did was impressive. Even from his earliest days as a player, Bob was a great leader. And you could see it in everything he did."

Oklahoma was coming off of three straight losing seasons, and there were a number of unknowns for the Sooners' next head coach. But Stoops embraced any and all challenges the program might present. And on December 1, 1998, he became the 21st head coach at OU.

Little did anyone know, it would be the beginning of something so special.

The Turning Point

When Bob Stoops took over as head coach prior to the 1999 season, Oklahoma fans were starving for positives. The Sooners had not posted a winning record in five years, and it seemed more like 500 years.

There were fans who expected miracles, but for the most part they just wanted to see a good product on the field. No more 51-7 losses to Texas A&M or embarrassing 73-21 setbacks against Nebraska.

Stoops talked about expectations and becoming contenders again, and then his team went out and delivered a 7-5 season that included the program's first bowl appearance since 1994. It proved to be the beginning of something special, and a year later the Sooners brought home their first national title in 15 seasons.

Players like quarterback Josh Heupel and defensive specialists Roy Williams, Rocky Calmus and Torrance Marshall led the revival.

Read, Recognize, React

Texas football fans still have nightmares about Oklahoma safety Roy Williams. At times, it's hard to close their eyes and not see him somehow adding to his legacy at the expense of their beloved Longhorns.

Williams seemingly made a habit of doing just that during his three seasons at OU.

The most memorable of Williams' clutch performances against Texas came in the 2001 contest, when he was the central character in a well-documented series of plays that decided the outcome. The biggest of those plays unfolded as a blitzing Williams leapt over a blocker to hit quarterback Chris Simms' arm, causing the ball to flutter into the awaiting arms of linebacker Teddy Lehman. Three steps later, Lehman was in the end zone, and OU was on its way to a 14-3 victory.

Josh Heupel. *Photo by Jerry Laizure*

"It was cool because it was such a big game," said Williams. "But I was over that after I talked to my mom that night. She said, 'Great job,' and that was that. It was time to move ahead."

Finally, the Monkey Jumps Off

There are so many challenges and expectations when following a legend in the coaching business. Gary Gibbs found that out the hard way from 1989-94 when he succeeded Oklahoma's all-time winningest coach, Barry Switzer.

Add in the fact that Gibbs took over a program hit hard by NCAA sanctions, and the hurdles his Sooners faced during that period were even larger than expected. Beating Texas was the biggest obstacle.

Gibbs' Oklahoma squad was a nationally ranked power for each of its first four meetings with Texas. And each time, despite being unranked, Texas sent the Sooners back north with a loss in tow.

It was a trend OU fans grew tired of in a hurry.

Finally in 1993, the 16th-ranked Sooners gave Gibbs a much-needed shot in the arm via a 38-17 victory in Dallas. But the celebration was short-lived. The following season, Texas returned to its winning ways with a 17-10 triumph. Gibbs was fired at the end of the year.

Asked what advice he would give incoming coach John Blake, Gibbs replied: "Beat Texas."

The Runt

When quarterback Nate Hybl arrived at Oklahoma after transferring from Georgia, one of the first people he ran into during off-season workouts was Quentin Griffin, a small unimposing-looking back from Aldine, Texas. Hybl was unimpressed, to say the least.

"I thought to myself 'Why in the world did OU waste a scholarship on this little runt?'" said Hybl. "He's 5-foot-2, 150

Quentin Griffin. *Photo by Jerry Laizure*

pounds with this big Afro. He wouldn't talk to you. I just couldn't believe he would be around very long."

When fall practice began prior to the 1999 season, Hybl found himself on the scout team and in the same backfield with Griffin. Slowly, his opinion changed.

"We'd be running scout team offense, and 'Q' would dice up the defense with some really nice runs. Still, I figured being as small as he was, he'd get swallowed up in a real game," said Hybl, who was sitting out due to NCAA rules.

Seven games into the season, OU's starting backfield had been so depleted by injuries that the coaching staff decided to bring Griffin out of redshirt. Over the final five games of '99, the diminutive back averaged 6.4 yards per carry in helping the Sooners earn an Independence Bowl berth.

"It was amazing. He was better in real games than he was in practice," laughed Hybl. "I couldn't have been more wrong about him. He turned out to be a great player."

Griffin finished his career fourth on OU's all-time rushing list. Not bad for a runt.

Watching and Waiting

Long before Bob Stoops became the 21st head coach at Oklahoma, he watched the Sooners develop and maintain a tradition that was second to none. As a defensive back at Iowa, he had played against Oklahoma in 1979, and even as a teenager, he watched Barry Switzer's Sooners on TV.

Like everybody else, Stoops was shocked to see a proud Oklahoma program plunge into mediocrity during the 1990s. From 1994-98, the Sooners failed to record a winning season, instead posting a combined mark of 23-34-1.

"I had felt all along and said that [Oklahoma] was a program that should be doing more than it was. I looked at the tradition and the history of winning and the recruiting base," said Stoops, pointing to the reasons he took the position. "I thought the potential was here to get back to those winning ways and to become a contender again."

In his first season as coach, Stoops led the Sooners to a 7-5 record and their first bowl appearance since 1994.

"Ace 92 Switch"

There have been 50 times in the history of Oklahoma football that a player has topped 100 receiving yards in a single game. Curtis Fagan's name is not on that list.

Bob Stoops. *Photo by Jerry Laizure*

That doesn't mean Fagan didn't do his share of catching the ball as a Sooner. He finished his career ranked fourth on OU's all-time receptions list. But his one big chance to hit the century mark slipped through his fingers, if you will.

It happened during his redshirt freshman season in 1999 as the Sooners were supplying Bedlam rival Oklahoma State with a 44-7 beating. Fagan hauled in a 73-yard touchdown pass and was sitting just 23 yards shy of 100 later in the third quarter.

"We were pretty much kicking their butts at that point, and Coach [Steve] Spurrier thought it was a good chance to get Curtis 100 yards," said OU receiver Damian Mackey. "I remember the play he sent in—ace 92 switch—which called for Curtis to run a corner route."

Fagan heard the play and lined up with most of his focus on running the proper route. Spurrier was a stickler about precise, crisp pass routes. Run a bad route and there would be hell to pay.

What Fagan did not notice as the Sooners came to the line of scrimmage was that OSU switched to a cover-2 defense. That meant he would probably get jammed at the line, which is exactly what happened.

"We rarely got touched that day, but Curtis couldn't break loose from his man," laughed Mackey. "There [Josh] Heupel is bird-dogging him for at least five seconds, and Curtis is flailing away trying to get free."

Heupel finally checked off to another receiver, and Fagan's shot at 100 yards was gone. Although almost a quarter of action was yet to be played, Fagan spent the rest of his afternoon standing next to Spurrier, listing everything he did wrong on that one play.

Close Call

Television crews camped out nearby and the phone never stopped ringing. Oklahoma had just beaten Arkansas in the 2002 Cotton Bowl, and what should have been a time of celebration for coach Bob Stoops and his family turned into several chaotic days of speculation and rumor.

At the heart of the matter was a job opening. Not just any job opening—the one Stoops' former boss, Steve Spurrier, had resigned at Florida three days earlier. Stoops served as Spurrier's defensive coordinator there for three seasons, and Florida came calling to see if OU's head man wanted to go back to the Sunshine State.

A season removed from the Sooners winning a national championship (in his second season), Stoops suddenly found himself in a fishbowl as the media, fans and the football world anxiously awaited his decision. He maintained his silence on the matter as he and his family agonized over the decision, which finally came during a Monday press conference.

"From time to time, people have choices in their lives as to what they want to do. I want to clarify and straighten out so many of the wrong rumors that have been out there recently," Stoops explained. "I feel committed and strong to what we're doing here at Oklahoma, about the strength of our program and where it's heading. I feel that is what's most important to me, continuing to develop this program at Oklahoma."

With those words came a collective sigh of relief in Soonerland.

Heart to Hearts

In the hours and days immediately after coach John Blake's removal as OU head coach at the end of the 1998 season, a revolt simmered among a large group of Sooner players, many of whom were angered by the move.

Roy Williams, Curtis Fagan, Andre Woolfolk, Damian Mackey and Josh Norman all decided to transfer to different schools at the end of the semester.

"We were all leaving and that was that," said Mackey, a freshman receiver who spent the season in redshirt. "Roy was going to UCLA. Josh was leaving. Andre, too. It pretty much had already been decided."

But before any papers were signed or any moving vans pulled up outside the Wilkinson Center, a message appeared on the lounge chalkboard. It read "Freshman meeting tonight."

Trent Smith, a freshman tight end from Clinton, Oklahoma, and a lifelong OU fan, wanted to talk to his classmates before they did anything rash. So he called the meeting and delivered a speech that potentially rescued Oklahoma from several more seasons of mediocrity.

"Trent came in and he was just about in tears," said Mackey. "He really spoke from the heart. He told us everything about the whole Sooner tradition and all of the great players who came before us. He went on about what OU football meant to him growing up."

Almost all of the players in the room that night had come in during OU's biggest recruiting weekend the previous season. They formed immediate bonds and were as tight as a class of complete strangers could be after such a short period of time.

And they listened as Smith listed all of the reasons why they should stay.

"Trent talked about how great our class could be and how close we had all become. He talked about the future and all of the possibilities it held," added Mackey. "That night, we decided we could be the class that helped get OU back to the way it was during the glory years.

"It's hard to admit an 18-year-old kid could influence your life like that, but Trent's speech was the reason we all stayed. It was one of those life-altering moments."

Two seasons later, life was altered again, as that group of freshman helped lead OU to its first national championship in 15 years.

Auntie V

Imagine Oklahoma football without Roy Williams. Definitely not a pretty picture. Oh, the Sooners would have still enjoyed a tremendous amount of success without the All-America safety, but it's hard to measure his full impact in terms of wins and losses.

Maybe the 2000 national championship would have remained a dream. Maybe not.

Either way, Sooner fans owe a debt of gratitude to Williams' aunt, Valetta Robinson. It was her persistence that opened the initial line of communication between her nephew and OU assistant coach Joe Dickinson. Otherwise, Williams may have ended up at UCLA or Stanford.

Dickinson was a part of head coach John Blake's much-maligned staff in 1997 when the Sooners were struggling to keep their heads above water in the new Big 12 Conference. They had recruited some decent talent to Norman, but for whatever reason, it wasn't showing on the field.

Robinson worked in OU's athletic cafeteria and promoted her nephew to the OU staff every chance she got. Dickinson took the bait and made Williams his primary target.

"My man Joe D. was relentless," said Williams, of the recruiting process. "All of the coaches played a big role in me coming to Oklahoma, but Coach Dickinson was probably the main guy."

Williams eventually signed with OU, but before he played a single down, Blake and his entire staff were fired.

Throwback

The extreme picture of a college jock from the 1980s. That's how teammates described OU lineman Matt O'Neal, he of the mustache, long hair, tattoos and brash personality. A native Californian, O'Neal looked better suited for the World Wrestling Federation.

"I was intimidated by him because he was this big, tough-looking guy who believed in the ranking system," said quarterback Nate Hybl. "If you were an underclassman, you didn't hang out with guys like him very often. He was just kind of a throwback-type player from the [1980s]."

Despite his less-than-conforming appearance, 6-foot-3, 265-pound O'Neal was a good football player. His hard work in the trenches earned him third team All-Big 12 honors as a senior.

Q, is that You?

A few days after the 2002 Cotton Bowl, in which Oklahoma beat Arkansas 10-3, running back Quentin Griffin barely had time to savor the fact he earned offensive MVP honors when he underwent surgery on his jaw. Griffin returned to school for the second semester shortly after and attended an OU basketball game on his first night back.

"I'm sitting at the game and here comes this kid who looks a little bit like Quentin, but he's a lot chubbier looking in the face. He sits down next to me, and I'm thinking it's some new recruit," said tight end Trent Smith. "We didn't speak or anything the entire game."

OU coach Bob Stoops had scheduled a team meeting later in the week and Smith was sitting in the film room talking to quarterback Nate Hybl when this same kid comes walking in.

"Nate keeps saying, 'That's Q, that's Q.' But I'm thinking there's no way. This guy doesn't look like Quentin in the face. He had the same build and hair, but that was it," said Smith.

The "new" kid walks over and sits down in the seat usually assigned to Griffin, and Smith is beside himself.

"Quentin? Is that you?" he asked.

"Yeah," replied Griffin.

"I'm sorry. I sat by you the entire game the other night and you didn't say a word," said Smith, noting that Griffin is one of the quietest guys on the team.

"Trent had me convinced it wasn't Q. And really, it didn't look like him. His face was still badly swollen from the surgery, which we knew nothing about at the time," added Hybl. "It was a weird deal, because I'm not sure many people recognized him for a while there."

Ninja Master

Mike Leach may have played a small role in the overall history of Oklahoma football, but his impact is undeniable. The first offensive coordinator under head coach Bob Stoops, Leach arrived with his own version of the West Coast spread offense and turned the Big 12 upside-down.

Opposing coaches either viewed Leach as either crazy or a genius, as he deployed an eccentric, shoot-from-the-hip style that pulled out all of the stops and kept the fans sitting on the edge of their seats.

"Coach Leach was the oddest character I've ever met in my life," confessed quarterback Nate Hybl. "But he was always the smartest dude in the building when it came to football. Unfortunately, not everybody got what he was trying to say because he was so out there."

Leach's offensive stylings were built around the pass, and quarterback Josh Heupel was the beneficiary, as he rewrote almost every OU single-season passing record during the 1999 season. The Sooners' multidimensional air attack included an unusual formation called the "Ninja," which created chaos by spreading players all over the field.

"Mike had no inhibitions when it came to calling plays. He wasn't afraid to do anything at any time in a game, no matter what the situation was," said tight end Trent Smith. "The fans loved it, but it was in contrast to a lot of coaches who are a lot more conventional and structured."

After only one season as OU's offensive coordinator, Leach took the head job at Texas Tech.

The Dentist

A lot of college quarterbacks ignore the NCAA rule that states "all players must wear a protective mouthpiece." Even though it is rarely flagged, failure to have one is a 15-yard penalty.

OU's Nate Hybl never wore one. He kept one on the sideline or stuck in his pants, but it made calling signals a bit awkward, so he opted to go without at the risk of getting a penalty.

Early during the 2001 Oklahoma-Texas A&M game, the head official began conversing with Hybl during breaks in the action when OU's offense was on the field. They chatted about a variety of things pertaining to the game before the official noticed Hybl was not using a mouthpiece.

"He asked me where my mouthpiece was and I made up a story about how I had forgotten it that series, but I'd get it next time I was on the sideline," recalled Hybl. "He looked at me and said, 'You do that, because not only is it against the rules, but I'm a dentist.'"

The official went on to explain why players should wear mouthpieces while Hybl listened intently. But that was the end of their conversation. The rest of the day, OU's quarterback did his best to avoid his company.

"Every time I ran by him I puffed out my mouth to make it look like I had a mouthpiece in," said Hybl, flashing a big smile. "Hey, I like my teeth as much as the next guy, but you've got to do what you've got to do."

Lost in Lubbock

The 1999 football season offered its share of twists and turns as Oklahoma ushered in a new era under first-year coach Bob Stoops. The biggest surprises came in the shape of a talented new quarterback and an offense that kept opponents on their heels with a wide-open, no-holds-barred mentality.

But the young Sooners struggled to finish off opponents in some big games, chalking it up to lack of experience in those situations, one of which occurred in Lubbock, Texas, against Texas Tech.

Oklahoma jumped out to a 21-13 halftime lead behind QB Josh Heupel, but could not put the Red Raiders away. The result was a 38-28 loss. But that was just the beginning of a very long night.

In the aftermath, Stoops greeted his team with a high-energy speech that did not spare any feelings. The Sooners had previously failed to hold leads against Notre Dame, Texas and Colorado, and emotions were running high as a result.

To make matters worse, as the players boarded the team bus, news came down that the charter flight scheduled to take them home that night was experiencing mechanical difficulties. The team ended back up at their hotel, waiting for news about the flight.

Finally, Stoops announced the flight had been canceled and they were going to make the seven-hour ride home on the bus that night. It was, to say the least, a no-nonsense trip back to Norman.

The capper came later when the team discovered receivers Curtis Fagan and Mike Jackson had been left behind at the hotel. The pair had fallen asleep in their room and missed the bus. Fagan had frantically tried to call several of his teammates via their cell phones—but no one was brave enough to have them turned on at that point.

Fagan and Jackson eventually hitched a ride with the parents of OU player Ryan Allen.

It turned out to be one of those forgettable trips that is hard to scrape from the memory.

Black October 2000

During the course of the last century, Oklahoma's football program has produced dozens upon dozens of victories in big games. In the midst of their run to the national title, the 2000 edition of the Sooners added an impressive list of victims to the list.

It was called "Black October" or "Red October," depending which media source you relied on, and it included a stretch of three games against No. 11 Texas, No. 2 Kansas State and top-ranked Nebraska.

Despite heading to Dallas with a 4-0 mark, Bob Stoops' OU squad had, at times, been inconsistent on both sides of the ball. General wisdom was if the Sooners emerged from the gauntlet with a 5-2 mark, it would be a good springboard into the rest of the season.

OU wasn't buying it.

The Sooners opened October with an amazing performance en route to a 63-14 thrashing of Texas. A week later, they stopped Kansas State's home winning streak at 25 with a 41-31 victory and then capped the month by rallying from a 14-0 deficit to upset No. 1 Nebraska, 31-14.

"That was as impressive of run as you'll ever see," said ESPN college football analyst Kirk Herbstreit. "They left little doubt about who the number-one team in the country was at that point."

Of course, the Sooners went on to win the 2000 national title, the seventh in their illustrious history.

The Script

OU offensive coordinator Mike Leach was always scheming in hopes of finding an edge over an opponent. During the 1999 season, the Sooners had opened with a 3-1 record and had a showdown with Texas next up on the schedule.

Like most coordinators, Leach always scripted out the Sooners' first dozen or so plays prior to the game and then used the list accordingly during the game. Well, he came up with an idea to plant a phony list of scripted plays where the Longhorns would find it.

If Texas fell for it, the plan might be good for a handful of big plays for his offense early in the game.

After Friday's practice at the Cotton Bowl, Leach left a laminated copy of the "fake" script laying on the bench where someone Longhorn would find it. They wouldn't know for sure until the opening series of the game.

The first play on the list was a reverse. And when quarterback Josh Heupel brought the Sooners to the line of scrimmage, cries of "Reverse, reverse" rang out from the Texas side of the field.

Of course, Leach had called for a fake reverse and OU racked up 20 yards on its initial snap. The phony script called for a run on the second play, but instead Heupel faked the handoff and hit Antwone Savage for a 44-yard touchdown pass.

It is impossible to know for sure how much the fake list factored into the early portion of the game, but the Sooners led 17-3 by the end of the opening quarter.

The Pick

Kyle Field is a madhouse, normally stuffed with almost 90,000 fanatics known as "The 12th man." Texas A&M opponents rarely play in a more hostile environment, and that is often a determining factor in the game's outcome.

Then again, nothing compares to "Sooner Magic," which is what Oklahoma used to sneak out of College Station with a 35-31 victory. The win kept the Sooners undefeated and their hopes Trailing 24-10 early in the fourth quarter, the Sooners were looking for any kind of spark to flip the momentum switch in their favor. And with the offense struggling much of the day, linebacker Torrance Marshall decided to take matters into his own hands. He did so by intercepting an A&M pass and returning it 41 yards for a touchdown.

OU eventually outscored the Aggies 22-7 in the final quarter and used a pair of spectacular defensive stands in the closing minutes to seal the victory.

"During the course of a season, a lot of football teams find themselves in a game where they are not playing their best football, and you've got to find a way to win," said quarterback Josh Heupel. "This football team found a way to win."

The Singing Quarterbacks

At any point before or after practice, the song "Midnight Train to Georgia" could be heard ringing out from the back portion of the OU locker room facility. That's where the singing trio was located.

Quarterbacks Josh Heupel, Nate Hybl and Patrick Fletcher formed their impromptu choir in an attempt to break the humdrum of their daily routine and the pressures that go with it. If one of them was having a bad day, a song was the perfect remedy.

"We'd get some serious tunes going back there. We had a lot of fun with it," said Hybl, who along with Fletcher and Jason White were backups to Heupel in 1999 and 2000. "I might come in in a bad mood, or Hype might be having a bad day—but we'd always turn it around with a song. More than anything it helped break up the monotony of practice."

South Dakota Kid

Aberdeen, South Dakota, is not known as a hotbed for collegiate football talent. But that's where Josh Heupel grew up and developed his skills as a young quarterback. From there, Heupel made stops at Weber State, Snow Junior College and finally, Oklahoma.

In his two seasons with the Sooners, the savvy southpaw blossomed from an unknown commodity into a Heisman Trophy candidate. He rewrote OU's record book as far as passing was concerned, and in the process became one of the most popular players to ever wear the crimson and cream.

"Josh Heupel is the complete package," said coach Bob Stoops. "He can do things physically in a great way and there aren't many quarterbacks out there with his instincts and overall intelligence."

After finishing second to Chris Weinke in the 2000 Heisman Trophy balloting, Heupel helped lead the Sooners to a victory over Florida State and Weinke. The 13-2 triumph earned OU its seventh national championship.

Celebrate the Heroes of Football
in These Other New and Recent Releases from Sports Publishing!

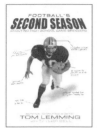

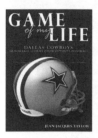
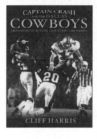